SHORTHAND

Pocket
Dictionary

Second Edition

Pitman

PITMAN PUBLISHING LIMITED
128 Long Acre, London WC2E 9AN

A Longman Group Company

First edition 1978
Second edition 1983
Reprinted 1983, 1984, 1985 (twice)

Printed in Great Britain by
Richard Clay (The Chaucer Press) Ltd,
Bungay, Suffolk

ISBN 0 273 01810 8

PREFACE

The Pitman 2000 Shorthand Pocket Dictionary is designed to provide, in a size suitable for pocket use, a guide to the shorthand outlines for the more common words in the English language. The shorthand outlines in this work are not always necessarily the only theoretically correct ones. The outlines show position writing and are given in vocalised shorthand. All the short forms and derivatives are shown italicized.

To Sonia,
All the best
from Barbara
x

6 Nov. 1987.

A

a		
aback'		
aban'don		
aban'doned		
aban'doning		
aban'donment		
abash'		
abashed'		
abate'		
aba'ted		
abate'ment		
abat'ing		
abattoir'		
ab'bot		
abbre'viate		
abbre'viated		
abbre'viating		
abbrevia'tion		
ab'dicate		
ab'dicated		
ab'dicating		
abdica'tion		
abdo'men		
abdom'inal		
abduct'		
abduct'ed		
abduct'ing		
abduc'tion		
aberra'tion		
abey'ance		
abhor'		
abhorred'		
abhor'rence		
abhor'rent		
abhor'ring		
abide'		
abid'ing		
abil'ity		
ab'ject		
ab'jectly		

ablaze'		
a'ble		
a'ble-bodied		
ablu'tion		
a'bly		
abnor'mal		
abnormal'ity		
aboard'		
abode'		
abol'ish		
abol'ished		
abol'ishing		
abol'ishment		
aboli'tion		
abom'inable		
abom'inate		
abom'inated		
abomina'tion		
aborig'inal		
abor'tive		
abound'		
abound'ed		
abound'ing		
about'		
above'		
abra'sion		
abreast'		
abridge'		
abridged'		
abridg'ing		
abridg'ment		
abroad'		
ab'rogate		
abroga'tion		
abrupt'		
abrupt'ly		
abrupt'ness		
ab'scess		
abscond'		
abscond'ed		

5

abscond'er	accel'erate
abscond'ing	accel'erated
ab'sence	accel'erating
{ab'sent, *a.*	accelera'tion
{absent', *v.*	accel'erator
absent'ed	{ac'cent, *n.*
absentee'	{accent', *v.*
ab'solute	accent'ed
ab'solutely	accent'ing
absolu'tion	accent'uate
absolve'	accent'uated
absorb'	accentua'tion
absorbed'	accept'
absorb'ent	accept'able
absorb'ing	accept'ance
absorp'tion	accept'ed
abstain'	accept'ing
abstain'er	ac'cess
abstain'ing	accessibil'ity
abste'mious	acces'sible
absten'tion	acces'sion
ab'stinence	ac'cessory
{abstract', *v.*	ac'cident
{ab'stract,	acciden'tal
a. & n.	acclaim'
abstract'ed	acclama'tion
abstract'ing	accli'matize
abstrac'tion	accli'matized
abstruse'	accli'matizing
absurd'	accom'modate
absurd'ity	accom'modated
absurd'ly	accom'modat-ing
abun'dance	accommoda'-tion
abun'dant	accom'panied
abun'dantly	accom'pani-ment
abuse'	accom'panist
abused'	accom'pany
abus'ing	accom'panying
abu'sive	accom'plice
abu'sively	accom'plish
abut'	accom'plished
abyss'	accom'plishing
academ'ic	accom'plish-ment
academ'ical	*accord'*
acad'emy	
accede'	
acced'ed	
acced'ing	

accord'ance	
accord'ed	
accord'ing	
accord'ingly	
accord'ion	
account'	
account'able	
account'ancy	
account'ant	
account'ed	
account'ing	
accred'ited	
accre'tion	
accrue'	
accrued'	
accru'ing	
accu'mulate	
accu'mulated	
accu'mulating	
accumula'tion	
accu'mulator	
ac'curacy	
ac'curate	
ac'curately	
accusa'tion	
accuse'	
accused'	
accus'ing	
accus'tom	
accus'tomed	
ace	
acerb'ity	
acet'ylene	
ache	
ached	
achieve'	
achieved'	
achieve'ment	
achiev'ing	
ach'ing	
ac'id	
acid'ity	
acidos'is	
acknowl'edge	
acknowl'edged	
acknowl'edging	
acknowl'edg-ment	

ac'me	
a'corn	
acous'tic	
acquaint'	
acquaint'ance	
acquaint'ed	
acquaint'ing	
acquiesce'	
acquies'cence	
acquire'	
acquired'	
acquire'ment	
acquir'ing	
acquisi'tion	
acquis'itive	
acquit'	
acquit'tal	
acquit'ted	
acquit'ting	
a'cre	
a'creage	
ac'rid	
acrimo'nious	
ac'robat	
acrobat'ic	
ac'ronym	
across'	
act	
act'ed	
act'ing	
actin'ium	
ac'tion	
ac'tionable	
ac'tivate	
ac'tive	
ac'tively	
activ'ity	
act'or	
act'ress	
act'ual	
act'ually	
act'uary	
acu'ity	
acu'men	
acute'	
acute'ly	
ad'age	
ad'amant	

adapt'	admin'istering
adaptabil'ity	admin'istrate
adapt'able	administra'-tion
adapta'tion	admin'istra-tive
adapt'ed	admin'istrator
adapt'ing	ad'mirable
add	ad'miral
ad'ded	ad'miralty
addict'	admira'tion
addic'ted	admire'
ad'ding	admired'
addi'tion	admir'er
addi'tional	admir'ing
address'	admir'ingly
addressed'	admis'sible
addressee'	admis'sion
address'ing	admit'
adept'	admit'tance
ad'equacy	admit'ted
ad'equate	admit'ting
ad'equately	admon'ish
adhere'	admon'ished
adhered'	admon'ishing
adhe'rence	admoni'tion
adhe'rent	adoles'cence
adhe'ring	adoles'cent
adhe'sion	adopt'
adhe'sive	adopt'ed
adhe'siveness	adopt'ing
adieu'	adop'tion
adja'cent	ador'able
adja'cently	adora'tion
ad'jective	adore'
adjoin'	ador'ing
adjoin'ing	adorn'
adjourn'	adorned'
adjourned'	adorn'ing
adjourn'ing	adorn'ment
adjourn'ment	adre'nal
adju'dicate	adren'alin
adjudica'tion	adult'
ad'junct	adul'terate
adjust'	adul'terated
adjust'ed	adultera'tion
adjust'ing	adult'hood
adjust'ment	advance'
admin'ister	
admin'istered	

advanced'	affect'
advance'ment	affecta'tion
advan'cing	affect'ed
advan'tage	affec'tion
advanta'geous	affec'tionate
advanta'ge- ously	affec'tionately
	affida'vit
adventi'tious	
adven'ture	affil'iate
adven'turer	affil'iated
adven'turess	affilia'tion
ad'verb	affirm'
ad'versary	affirm'ative
ad'verse	affirmed'
ad'versely	affirm'ing
adver'sity	{affix', v.
ad'vertise	{af'fix, n.
ad'vertised	affixed'
adver'tise- ment	affix'ing
	afflict'
ad'vertiser	afflict'ed
ad'vertising	afflict'ing
advice'	afflic'tion
advisabil'ity	af'fluently
advis'able	afford'
advise'	afford'ed
advised'	afford'ing
advis'edly	afforesta'tion
advis'er	affront'
advis'ing	affront'ed
advis'ory	afloat'
ad'vocacy	afore'said
ad'vocate, n.	afraid'
ad'vocate, v.	afresh'
ad'vocated	Af'rican
ae'rial	Afrikaans'
aerobat'ics	Afrikan'der
aer'obus	aft'er
aer'odrome	aft'ermath
aer'ofoil	afternoon'
aeronau'tic	aft'erwards
aer'oplane	again'
aesthet'ic	against'
aesthet'ics	age
affabil'ity	a'ged
af'fable	a'gency
af'fably	agen'da
affair'	a'gent

aggrand'ize-ment	
ag'gravate	
ag'gravated	
ag'gravating	
aggrava'tion	
ag'gregate	
ag'gregated	
ag'gregating	
aggrega'tion	
aggres'sion	
aggress'ive	
aggress'or	
aggrieve'	
aggrieved'	
aghast'	
ag'ile	
agil'ity	
ag'itate	
ag'itated	
ag'itating	
agita'tion	
ag'itator	
agnos'tic	
ago'	
ag'onizing	
ag'ony	
agree'	
agree'able	
agreed'	
agree'ing	
agree'ment	
agricul'tural	
ag'riculture	
agricul'turist	
aground'	
a'gue	
ah	
ahead'	
aid	
aid'ed	
aide-mém'oire	
aid'ing	
ail	
ailed	
ail'ing	

ail'ment	
aim	
aimed	
aim'ing	
aim'less	
aim'lessly	
aim'lessness	
air	
air'borne	
air'craft	
air'field	
air'force	
air'-hole	
air'-lift	
air'line	
air'mail	
air'minded	
air'plane	
air'port	
air-shaft	
air'ship	
air'strip	
air'tight	
air'way	
air'worthi'ness	
air'worthy	
aisle	
akin'	
à la carte'	
alac'rity	
alarm'	
alarmed'	
alarm'ing	
alarm'ingly	
alas'	
al'bum	
al'cohol	
alcohol'ic	
al'derman	
ale	
alert'	
alert'ness	
al'gebra	
a'lias	
al'ibi	
a'lien	
a'lienate	
a'lienated	

a'lienating		allud'ed	
aliena'tion		allud'ing	
alight'		allure'	
alight'ed		allur'ing	
alight'ing		allur'ingly	
align', aline'		allu'sion	
align'ment		allu'via	
alike'		al'ly	
aliment'ary		al'manac	
al'imony		almight'y	
alive'		al'mond	
al'kali		al'most	
al'kaline		aloft'	
all		alone'	
allay'		along'	
allayed'		along'side	
allay'ing		aloof'	
allega'tion		aloud'	
allege'		al'phabet	
alleged'		alphabet'ic	
alle'giance		alphabet'ical	
alleg'ing		Alp'ine	
all'ergy		*al'ready*	
alle'viate		al'so	
alle'viated		al'tar	
alle'viating		al'ter	
allevia'tion		altera'tion	
al'ley		alterca'tion	
al'leyway		al'tered	
alli'ance		al'tering	
al'lied		al'ternate, *v.*	
al'lies		altern'ate, *a.*	
al'locate		al'ternated	
al'located		altern'ately	
al'locating		al'ternating	
alloca'tion		alter'native	
allot'		altern'atively	
allot'ment		al'ternator	
allot'ropism		*although'*	
allot'ted		al'titude	
allot'ting		*altogeth'er*	
allow'		al'truism	
allow'able		altruis'tic	
allow'ance		alumin'ium	
allowed'		alu'minum	
allow'ing		*al'ways*	
alloy'		am	
allude'		amal'gamate	

amal'gamated
amal'gamating
amalgama'tion
amanuen'sis
amass'
amassed'
amass'ing
am'ateur
amaze'
amazed'
amaze'ment
amaz'ing
amaz'ingly
Am'azon
ambas'sador
am'ber
ambigu'ity
ambig'uous
ambig'uously
ambi'tion
ambi'tious
ambi'tiously
ambiv'alence
ambiv'alent
am'bulance
am'bush
ame'liorate
ameliora'tion
amen'
ame'nable
ame'nably
amend'
amend'ed
amend'ment
amen'ity
Amer'ican
Amer'icanism
a'miable
am'icable
am'icably
amid'
amidst'
amiss'
am'ity
ammo'nia
ammuni'tion
amoe'bic
amok'

among'
amongst'
amo'ral
amoral'ity
amortiza'tion
amor'tize
amor'tizement
amount'
amount'ed
amount'ing
amp'
amper'age
amphib'ian
amphithe'atre
am'ple
amplifica'tion
am'plified
am'plifier
am'plify
am'plifying
am'ply
am'poule
am'putate
am'putated
am'putating
amputa'tion
amuse'
amused'
amuse'ment
amus'ing
an
anach'ronism
anae'mia
anaem'ic
anaesthet'ic
analges'ic
anal'ogous
anal'ogy
an'alyse
an'alysed
an'alysing
anal'ysis
an'alyst
analyt'ic
analyt'ical
an'archist
an'archy
anath'ema

anatom'ical

anat'omy

an'cestor

ances'tral

anch'or

anch'ored

anch'oring

an'cient

and

an'ecdote

ane'mic

   anae'mic

anesthet'ic

   anaesthet'ic

anew'

an'gel

angel'ic

an'ger

an'gered

an'gle

Ang'lophil

Ang'lophile

Ang'lophobe

ango'ra

an'grily

an'gry

an'guish

an'gular

angular'ity

an'iline

an'imal

an'imate

an'imated

an'imating

anima'tion

animos'ity

an'iseed

an'kle

an'nals

annex'

annexa'tion

annexed'

annex'ing

anni'hilate

anni'hilated

anni'hilating

annihila'tion

anniver'sary

an'notate

an'notated

an'notating

annota'tion

announce'

announced'

announce'-
   ment

announc'er

announc'ing

annoy'

annoy'ance

annoyed'

annoy'ing

an'nual

an'nually

annu'ity

annul'

annul'ling

an'num

anom'alous

anom'aly

anonym'ity

anon'ymous

anon'ymously

anoph'eles

anoth'er

an'swer

an'swerable

an'swered

an'swering

antag'onism

antag'onist

antagonist'ic

antag'onize

Antarc'tic

antece'dent

an'tedate

an'tedated

antenat'al

an'them

anthol'ogist

anthol'ogy

an'thracite

an'thrax

anti-air'craft	appalled'	
antibiot'ic	appall'ing	
an'tic	appara'tus	
antic'ipate	appar'el	
antic'ipated	appa'rent	
antic'ipating	appa'rently	
anticipa'tion	appeal'	
an'tidote	appealed'	
antihist'amine	appeal'ing	
an'tiquated	appear'	
antique'	appear'ance	
antiq'uity	appeared'	
anti-semit'ic	appear'ing	
antisep'tic	appease'	
antith'esis	appel'lant	
anti-vivisec'tion	appel'late	
ant'ler	appella'tion	
an'vil	append'	
anxi'ety	append'age	
anx'ious	append'ed	
anx'iously	appen'dices	
an'y	appendici'tis	
an'ybody	append'ing	
an'yhow	appen'dix	
an'yone	appen'dixes	
an'ything	appertain'	
an'ytime	appertained'	
an'yway	appertain'ing	
an'ywhere	ap'petite	
apart'	ap'petize	
apart'heid	ap'petizing	
apart'ment	applaud'	
apathet'ic	applaud'ed	
ap'athy	applaud'ing	
ape'ritif	applause'	
ap'erture	ap'ple	
a'pex	appli'ance	
aph'orism	ap'plicable	
aphrodis'iac	ap'plicant	
apiece'	applica'tion	
apologet'ic	applied'	
apolo'gia	apply'	
apol'ogize	apply'ing	
apol'ogized	appoint'	
apol'ogizing	appoint'ed	
apol'ogy	appoint'ing	
apos'tle	appoint'ment	
appal'		

appor'tion		A'pril	
appor'tioned		a'pron	
appor'tioning		apropos'	
appor'tion-ment		apt	
ap'posite		apt'itude	
apprais'al		apt'ly	
appraise'		apt'ness	
appraised'		a'qualung	
appre'ciable		aquamarine'	
appre'ciate		a'qua-planing	
appre'ciated		aqua'rium	
appre'ciating		aquat'ic	
apprecia'tion		a'queduct	
appre'ciative		Ar'ab	
apprehend'		Ara'bian	
apprehend'ed		Ar'abic	
apprehend'ing		ar'able	
apprehen'sion		ar'biter	
apprehen'sive		arb'itrage	
appren'tice		ar'bitrarily	
appren'ticed		ar'bitrary	
appren'tice-ship		ar'bitrate	
approach'		ar'bitrated	
approach'able		ar'bitrating	
approached'		arbitra'tion	
approach'ing		ar'bitrator	
approba'tion		arbor'eal	
appro'priate		ar'bour, ar'bor	
appro'priated		arc	
appro'priately		arcade'	
appro'priate-ness		arch	
		archa'ic	
appro'priating		archbish'op	
appropria'tion		ar'chitect	
approv'al			
approve'		architect'ural	
approved'			
approv'ing		ar'chitecture	
approv'ingly			
approx'imate		Arc'tic	
approx'imated		ar'dent	
approx'imately		ar'dently	
approx'imat-ing		ar'dour, ar'dor	
		ar'duous	
approxima'-tion		*are*	
		a'rea	
		are'na	
		Ar'gentine	
		ar'gosy	

ar'gue	arrest'ed
ar'gued	arrest'ing
ar'guing	arri'val
ar'gument	arrive'
argumen'ta-tive	arrived'
ar'id	arriv'ing
arid'ity	ar'rogance
aright'	ar'rogant
arise'	ar'rogantly
aris'en	ar'row
aris'ing	ar'senal
aristoc'racy	ar'senic
ar'istocrat	ar'son
aristocrat'ic	art
arith'metic	ar'tery
arithmet'ical	arte'sian
arm	art'ful
Armagedd'on	ar'ticle
ar'mament	art'ifact
ar'mature	art'ifice
arm'chair	artifi'cial
armed	artil'lery
arm'ing	ar'tisan
arm'istice	art'ist
ar'mour, ar'mor	artist'ic
arms	ar'tistry
ar'my	art'less
aro'ma	as
arose'	asbes'tos
around'	ascend'
arouse'	ascen'dancy
aroused'	ascend'ency
arous'ing	ascertain'
arraign'	ascertained'
arraigned'	ascet'ic
arrange'	ascor'bic
arranged'	ascribe'
arrange'ment	ascribed'
arrang'ing	ascrib'ing
array'	ash
arrayed'	ashamed'
arrear'	ashore'
arrears'	A'sian
arrest'	Asiat'ic
	aside'
	asinin'ity
	ask
	askance'

asked		assign'	
asleep'		assigned'	
as'pect		assignee'	
asper'sion		assign'ment	
as'phalt		assignor'	
asphyxia'tion		assigns'	
aspi'rant		assim'ilate	
as'pirate, n.		assim'ilated	
as'pirate, v.		assim'ilating	
aspira'tion		assimila'tion	
aspire'		assist'	
aspired'		assist'ance	
aspir'in		assist'ant	
aspir'ing		assist'ed	
assail'		assist'ing	
assail'ant		assize'	
assailed'		assiz'es	
assail'ing		asso'ciate	
assas'sin		asso'ciated	
assas'sinate		asso'ciating	
assas'sinated		associa'tion	
assault'		assort'	
assault'ed		assort'ed	
assault'ing		assort'ing	
assay'		assort'ment	
assayed'		assuage'	
assay'er		assume'	
assay'ing		assumed'	
assem'ble		assum'ing	
assem'bled		assump'tion	
assem'bling		assur'ance	
assem'bly		assure'	
assent'		assured'	
assent'ed		assur'edly	
assent'ing		assur'ing	
assert'		as'ter	
assert'ed		as'terisk	
assert'ing		asth'ma	
asser'tion		astir'	
assess'		aston'ish	
assessed'		aston'ished	
assess'ing		aston'ishing	
assess'ment		aston'ishment	
assess'or		astound'	
as'sets		astound'ed	
assidu'ity		astrakhan'	
assid'uous			
assid'uously			

astray'	
astrin'gent	
as'trodome	
astrol'ogy	
as'tronaut	
astronaut'ics	
astron'omer	
astron'omy	
astute'	
asun'der	
asy'lum	
at	
ate	
a'theist	
ath'lete	
athlet'ic	
athlet'ics	
Atlan'tic	
At'las, at'las	
at'mosphere	
atmospher'ic	
atmosphe'rics	
at'om	
at'omizer	
aton'al	
atone'	
atoned'	
atone'ment	
atro'cious	
atro'ciously	
atroc'ity	
at'rophy	
attach'	
attached'	
attach'ing	
attach'ment	
attack'	
attacked'	
attack'ing	
attain'	
attain'able	
attained'	
attain'ing	
attain'ment	
attempt'	
attempt'ed	
attempt'ing	
attend'	

attend'ance	
attend'ant	
attend'ed	
attend'ing	
atten'tion	
atten'tive	
atten'tively	
atten'uate	
attest'	
attesta'tion	
attest'ed	
attest'er, attest'or	
attest'ing	
at'tic	
attire'	
attired'	
at'titude	
attor'ney	
Attor'ney-General	
attract'	
attract'ed	
attract'ing	
attrac'tion	
attract'ive	
attract'ively	
attrib'utable	
{at'tribute, n.	
{attrib'ute, v.	
attrib'uted	
attrib'uting	
au'burn	
auc'tion	
auc'tioneer'	
auda'cious	
auda'ciously	
audac'ity	
audibil'ity	
au'dible	
au'dience	
au'dio	
au'dit	
au'dited	
au'diting	
au'ditor	
audito'rium	
aught	

augment'	automot'ive
augment'ed	auto-sugges'tion
augment'ing	au'tumn
au'gur	autum'nal
au'gured	auxil'iary
{Au'gust, *n.*	avail'
{august', *adj.*	avail'able
aunt	availed'
au'ral	avail'ing
au'spices	av'alanche
auspi'cious	av'arice
	avari'cious
auspi'ciously	avenge'
	avenged'
Australa'sian	av'enue
Austra'lian	aver'
Aus'trian	av'erage
aut'archy	av'eraged
authen'tic	av'eraging
authen'ticate	averse'
authen'ticated	aver'sion
authentic'ity	avert'
au'thor	avert'ed
au'thoress	avert'ing
authoritar'ian	avia'tion
authori-	a'viator
tar'ianism	a'viatrix
author'itative	av'id
author'ita-	av'idly
tively	avoca'do
author'ity	avoca'tion
authoriza'tion	avoid'
au'thorize	avoid'able
au'thorized	avoid'ance
au'thorizing	avoid'ed
au'thorship	avoid'ing
aut'o	avow'
autobiograph'-	avow'al
ical	await'
autobiog'raphy	await'ed
autoc'racy	await'ing
au'tocrat	awake'
autocrat'ic	awa'ken
au'tograph	awa'kened
aut'omate	awa'kening
automat'ic	award'
automa'tion	award'ed
autom'aton	
automobile'	

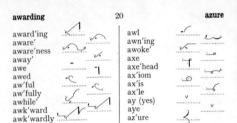

award'ing	awl
aware'	awn'ing
aware'ness	awoke'
away'	axe
awe	axe'head
awed	ax'iom
aw'ful	ax'is
aw'fully	ax'le
awhile'	ay (yes)
awk'ward	aye
awk'wardly	az'ure

B

bab'ble
ba'by
bab'y-sitt'er
bach'elor
bacil'lus
back
back'ben'cher
back'bone
back'chat
back'cloth
back'fire
back'ground
back'log
back'marker
back'num'ber
back'scratch'er
back'wards
ba'con
bacte'ria
bacteriol'ogist
bad
bade
badge
bad'ly
baf'fle
baf'fled
baf'fling
bag
bag'gage
bag'pipe
bail
bailed
bai'liff
bait
bait'ing
bake
bak'er
bak'ery
bak'ing
bal'ance

bal'anced
bal'ance-sheet
bal'ancing
bal'cony
bald
bald'headed
bald'ly
bale
baled
balk
ball
bal'lad
bal'last
ballerin'a
balletomane'
balletoma'nia
balloon'
bal'lot
bal'loted
ballyhoo'
balm'y
bal'sa
bamboo'
ban
bana'na
band
band'age
band'aging
band'ed
band'master
band'saw
band'wag'on
bang
banged
ban'ish
ban'ished
ban'ishment
bank
bank'book
banked

21

bank'er	
bank'ing	
bank'rupt	
bank'ruptcy	
ban'ner	
ban'quet	
ban'ter	
bap'tism	
Bap'tist	
baptize'	
baptized'	
bar	
barathe'a	
barbar'ic	
bar'barous	
bar'ber	
barb'itone	
barbiturate'	
bare	
bared	
bare'faced	
bare'ly	
bar'est	
bar'gain	
bar'gaining	
barge	
bar'ing	
bark	
bark'ing	
bar'ley	
barn	
barom'eter	
baromet'ric	
baroque'	
bar'rage	
barred	
bar'rel	
bar'ren	
barricade'	
barrica'ded	
barrica'ding	
bar'rier	
bar'ring	
bar'row	
bar'ter	

bar'tered	
bar'tering	
bas'cule	
base	
base'ball	
based	
base'less	
base'ment	
bash'ful	
ba'sic	
bas'ically	
ba'sin	
ba'sing	
ba'sis	
bas'ket	
bas'ketball	
bat	
batch	
bath	
bathe	
bath'er	
bath'ing	
bath'room	
bath'yscaphe	
bath'ysphere	
bat'tery	
bat'tle	
bat'tleship	
baulk	
baux'ite	
Bava'rian	
bay	
bazaar	
be	
beach	
beach'- comber	
bea'con	
bead	
beak	
beam	
beamed	
bean	
bean'o	
bear	
bear'able	
beard	
beard'ed	

bear'er	befriend'ed
bear'ing	befriend'ing
beast	beg
beast'ly	began
beat	beg'gar
beat'en	beg'ging
beat'ing	begin'
beau'tified	begin'ner
beau'tiful	begin'ning
beau'tify	begrudge'
beau'tifying	begrudg'ing
beau'ty	beguile'
bea'ver	beguiled'
became'	begun'
because'	behalf'
beck'on	behave'
beck'oned	beha'ving
beck'oning	behav'iour,
become'	behav'ior
becom'ing	behav'iourism
bed	behav'iourist
bed'ding	beheld'
bed'pan	behind'
bedrag'gle	behold'
bedrag'gled	behoove'
bed'rock	beige
bed'room	*be'ing*
bed'sit'ter	belat'ed
bed'spread	bel'fry
bed'stead	Bel'gian
bed'time	belief'
bee	believ'able
beech	believe'
beef	believed'
bee'hive	believ'er
been	believ'ing
beer	belit'tle
beet	belit'tled
beet'le	bell
befall'	bellig'erent
befal'len	bel'low
befell'	bel'lowing
befit	bell'push
befit'ted	belong
befit'ting	belonged'
before'	belong'ing
*before'*hand	beloved'
befriend'	belov'ed

below'		best	
belt		bestow'	
bench		bestowed'	
bend		bet	
bend'able		bête-noire	
bend'ing		betray'	
beneath'		betray'al	
benedic'tion		betroth'	
benefac'tor		betroth'al	
ben'efice		betrothed'	
benef'icence		bet'ter	
benef'icent		bet'tering	
benef'icently		bet'terment	
		bet'ting	
benefi'cial		between'	
benefi'ciary		betwixt'	
ben'efit		bev'el	
ben'efited		bev'elled,	
ben'efiting		bev'eled	
benev'olence		bev'erage	
benev'olent		beware'	
benign'		bewil'der	
benig'nant		bewil'dered	
benign'ly		bewil'dering	
bent		bewil'derment	
ben'zine		beyond'	
bequeath'		bian'nual	
bequeathed'		bi'as	
bequeath'ing		bi'ased	
bequest'		Bi'ble	
bereave'		Bib'lical	
bereaved'		bibliog'raphy	
bereave'ment		bi'cycle	
bereft'		bid	
ber'et		bid'der	
ber'ry		bid'ding	
ber'serk		bien'nial	
berth		bifo'cal	
beseech'		bifo'cals	
beseech'ing		big	
beset'		big'amist	
beset'ting		big'amous	
beside'		big'amy	
besides'		big'ger	
besiege'		big'gest	
besieg'ing		big'ot	
		big'oted	
		big'otry	

bikin'i	
biling'ualism	
bil'ious	
bil'iousness	
bill	
billed	
bil'let	
bill'iards	
bil'lion	
bil'low	
bimet'allism, bimet'alism	
bind	
bind'er	
bind'ery	
bind'ing	
bing'o	
binoc'ular	
biochem'ical	
biochem'ist	
biochem'istry	
biog'rapher	
biograph'ic	
biograph'ical	
biog'raphy	
biolog'ical	
biol'ogy	
birch	
bird	
bird's'-eye	
birth	
birth'-control'	
birth'day	
birth'mark	
birth'place	
birth'rate	
birth'right	
bis'cuit	
bisect'	
bisect'ed	
bisect'ing	
bish'op	
bis'muth	
bit	
bite	
bit'ing	

bit'ten	
bit'ter	
bit'terness	
bitu'minous	
bizarre'	
black	
black'berry	
black'bird	
black'board	
black'en	
black'ened	
black'ening	
black'guard	
black'mail	
black'smith	
blad'der	
blade	
blame	
blamed	
blame'less	
blame'worthy	
blank	
blank'et	
blaspheme'	
blasphemed'	
blas'phemous	
blas'phemy	
blast	
blast'ed	
blast'ing	
bla'tant	
blaze	
blazed	
blaz'er	
bleach	
bleach'ing	
bleak	
bled	
bleed	
bleed'ing	
blem'ish	
blend	
blend'ed	
bless	
blessed	
bless'ed	
bless'ing	
blest	

blew	blun'der
blight	blun'dered
blight'ed	blun'dering
blight'ing	blunt
blind	blunt'ed
blind'ed	blunt'ly
blind'fold	blur
blind'folded	blurred
blind'ing	blur'ring
blind'ly	blurt
blind'ness	blurt'ed
blindspot	blush
blink'ered	blushed
bliss	blush'ing
bliss'ful	blus'ter
bliss'fulness	blus'tered
blis'ter	blus'tering
blis'tered	blus'tery
blis'tering	board
blithe	board'ed
blitz	board'er
bliz'zard	board'ing
block	board'ing-
blockade'	house
blockad'ed	boast
blockad'ing	boast'ed
blocked	boast'ful
block'head	boast'fulness
blond, blonde	boast'ing
blood	boat
blood'-group	boat'house
blood'shed	boat'swain
bloom	bob
bloomed	bobbed
blos'som	bob'sleigh
blos'somed	bod'ily
blot	bod'y
blotch	bod'yguard
blot'ter	boff'in
blouse	bo'gus
blow	Bohe'mian
blow'ing	boil
blow'lamp	boiled
blown	boil'er
blue	bois'terous
blue'berry	bois'terously
blue'-chip	bold
bluff	bold'er

bold'ly	
bold'ness	
Bol'shevik	
bol'ster	
bol'stered	
bol'stering	
bolt	
bolt'ed	
bomb	
bom'bard, *n.*	
bombard', *v.*	
bombard'ed	
bombard'ing	
bombard'ment	
bombast'ic	
bomb'proof	
bomb'shell	
bond	
bond'age	
bond'ed	
bond'holder	
bone	
bon'fire	
bon'net	
bo'nus	
book	
book'binder	
book'binding	
book'case	
book'-keeper	
book'-keeping	
book'let	
book'seller	
book'shelf	
book'stall	
book'store	
book'worm	
boom	
boomed	
boon	
boost	
boost'er	
boot	
booth	
bor'der	
bor'dering	
bor'derline	
bore	

bored	
bore'dom	
bo'ring	
born	
borne	
bor'ough	
bor'row	
bor'rowed	
bor'rower	
bor'rowing	
bos'om	
boss	
bot'anist	
bot'any	
both	
both'er	
both'ered	
both'ering	
bot'tle	
bot'tleneck	
bot'tling	
bot'tom	
boudoir'	
bough	
bought	
boul'der	
boul'evard	
bounce	
bounced	
bounc'ing	
bound	
bound'ary	
bound'ed	
bound'ing	
bound'less	
boun'tiful	
boun'ty	
bouquet'	
bourgeois'	
bour'geois	
bout	
boutique'	
bow (part of a violin; a weapon)	
bow (part of a ship; to bend the body)	

bowed	
bow'els	
bow'er	
bow'ing	
bowl	
bowled	
bowl'er	
bow'line	
box	
boxed	
box'er	
box'-office	
boy	
boy'cott	
boy'hood	
boy'ish	
boy'ishly	
bra	
brace	
braced	
brace'let	
bra'ces	
brack'et	
brack'eted	
brag	
bragged	
braid	
braid'ed	
braid'ing	
Braille	
brain	
brain'less	
brain'wash	
brain'wave	
brake	
branch	
branch'ing	
brand	
brand'ed	
bran'dish	
bran'dished	
bran'dy	
brass	
brass'erie	
brass'ière	
brava'do	
brave	
brave'ly	

brav'ery	
brav'est	
brawl	
brawled	
brawn	
bra'zen	
Brazil'ian	
breach	
bread	
breadth	
bread'winner	
break	
break'able	
break'age	
break'down	
break'fast	
break'ing	
break'neck	
break'water	
breast	
breath	
breathe	
breath'less	
bred	
breech	
breed	
breed'er	
breed'ing	
breeze	
breez'y	
breth'ren	
brev'ity	
brew	
brew'ing	
bribe	
bribed	
brib'ery	
brick	
brick'layer	
brick'work	
brick'yard	
bri'dal	
bride	
bridge	
bri'dle	
bri'dled	
brief	
brief'est	

brief'ly	bronzed
brigade'	bronz'ing
brigadier'	brooch
brig'and	brood
bright	brood'ed
bright'en	brood'ing
bright'er	brook
bright'ly	broom
bright'ness	broth
bril'liance	broth'er
bril'liancy	broth'erhood
bril'liant	broth'er-*in*-law
bril'liantly	brought
brim	brow
brim'ful	brown
brine	bruise
bring	bruised
brink	brunette'
brisk	brunt
bris'tle	brush
bris'tled	brushed
Britan'nic	brush'wood
Brit'ish	brusque
brit'tle	bru'tal
brit'tleness	brutal'ity
broach	bru'tally
broach'ing	brute
broad	bub'ble
broad'cast	bub'bled
broad'caster	buck
broad'casting	buck'et
broad'en	buc'kle
broad'er	buck'ram
broad'ly	buck'wheat
broad'mind'ed	bucol'ic
brocade'	bud
brocad'ed	bud'ding
bro'chure	budg'erigar'
brogue	budg'et
broke	budg'eting
bro'ken	buff
brok'en-	buf'falo
heart'ed	buf'fet
bro'ker	buf'feted
bro'mide	bug'bear
bron'chial	bug'gy
bronchi'tis	bu'gle
bronze	bu'gler

build	burg'lary
build'er	bur'ial
build'ing	bur'ied
built	burlesque'
bulb	bur'ly
bulge	burn
bulk	burned
bulk'y	burn'er
bull	burn'ing
bull'doze	burnt
bull'dozer	bur'row
bul'let	bur'rowed
bul'letin	bur'rowing
bul'let-proof	burst
bul'lied	burst'ing
bul'lion	bur'y
bul'lock	bur'ying
bul'ly	bus
bul'lying	bush
bul'wark	bush'el
bump	bus'ier
bumped	bus'iest
bump'er	bus'ily
bump'ing	bus'iness
bump'tious	bus'inesslike
bump'tious-	bus'inessman'
ness	bust
bun	bus'tle
bunch	bus'tled
bun'dle	bus'y
bun'galow	*but*
bun'gle	butch'er
bunk	but'ler
bunk'er	butt
buoy'ancy	butt'ed
buoy'ant	but'ter
buoy'antly	but'ton
buoyed	but'tonhole
bur'den	buy
	buy'er
bur'densome	buy'ing
	buzz
bureau'	by, bye
bur'eaucrat	by'pass
bureaucrat'ic	by'-prod'uct
burg	by'stander
burg'lar	by'word

C

cab
cab'bage
cab'in
cab'inet
ca'ble
ca'blegram
cack'le
cadet'
Caesa'rean
ca'fé
cafete'ria
cage
cajole'
cake
caked
calam'itous
calam'ity
cal'culable
cal'culate
cal'culated
cal'culating
calcula'tion
Caledo'nian
cal'endar,
    cal'ender
cal'endered
calf
cal'ibre,
    cal'iber
cal'ico
calk, caulk
call
called
call'er
call'-girl
call'ing
cal'lous
cal'lousness
calm
calmed

calm'er
calm'ly
cal'orie
calum'niate
cal'umny
calyp'so
camaraderie
cam'ber
cam'bric
came
cam'el
cam'eo
cam'era
cam'ouflage
camp
campaign'
camp'-bed
camped
cam'phor
cam'phorated
camp'ing
cam'pus
can
Cana'dian
canal'
can'apé
can'ary
can'cel
cancella'tion
can'celled
can'celling
can'cer
can'did
can'didacy
can'didate
can'didly
can'dle
can'dlestick

31

can'dour, can'dor	
can'dy	
cane	
can'ine	or
can'ister	
can'ker	
can'kered	
canned	
can'nery	
can'ning	
can'non	
can'not	
canoe'	
can'on	
cañ'on	
can'opy	
cant	
cantan'kerous	
canteen'	
can'ter	
can'tered	
can'ton	
can'vas, *adj., n.*	
can'vass, *v.*	
can'vassed	
can'vasser	
can'yon	
cap	
capabil'ity	
ca'pable	
ca'pably	
capa'cious	
capac'itance	
capac'itor	
capac'ity	
cape	
cap'ital	
cap'italism	
cap'italist	
capitalis'tic	
capitaliza'tion	
cap'italize	
Cap'itol	
capit'ulate	
capitula'tion	
caprice'	

capri'cious	
capsize'	
capsized'	
cap'stan	
cap'sule	
cap'tain	
cap'tion	
cap'tivate	
cap'tivated	
captiva'tion	
cap'tive	
captiv'ity	
cap'tor	
cap'ture	
cap'tured	
car	
car'amel	
car'at	
car'avan	
car'bide	
carbohy'drate	
carbol'ic	
car'bon	
carbon'ic	
car'bonizer	
car'burate	
car'burettor, car'buretter	
car'cass	
carcinogen'ic	
card	
card'board	
car'diac	
car'digan	
car'dinal	
card'-in'dex	
car'diogram	
car'diograph	
care	
cared	
career'	
career'ist	
care'free	
care'ful	
care'fully	
care'less	
care'lessness	
caress'	

caressed'	cas'tigate
car'et	castiga'tion
care'worn	cast'ing
car'go	cast'-iron
car'icature	cas'tle
car'icatured	cas'tor
car'ing	cas'tor oil
car'mine	cas'ual
carna'tion	cas'ualism
car'nival	cas'ually
carn'ivore	cas'uals
carniv'orous	cas'ualty
car'ol	cat
carp	cat'aclysm
car'penter	cat'alogue
car'pentry	cat'apult
car'pet	cat'aract
car'riage	catarrh'
car'ried	catarrh'al
car'rier	catas'trophe
car'rot	catastroph'ic
car'ry	catch
car'rying	catch'-phrase
cart	catch'ing
cart'age	cat'echism
carte blanche'	categor'ical
cart'ed	cat'egory
car'ton	ca'ter
cartoon'	ca'tering
cartoon'ist	cat'erpillar
car'tridge	cathe'dral
carve	Cath'olic,
carved	cath'olic
carv'er	Cathol'icism
carv'ing	cat'tle
cascade'	caught
case	caul'dron
cash	cau'liflower
cashed	caulk
cashier'	cause
cash'ing	caused
cash'mere	caus'ing
cash'-register	caus'tic
cask	cau'terize
cas'ket	cau'tion
cassette	cau'tionary
cast	cau'tioned
caste	cau'tioning

cau'tious		cen'tigrade	
cau'tiously		cen'tral	
cavalcade'		centraliza'tion	
cavalier'		cen'tralize	
cav'alry		cen'tralized	
cave		cen'tre	
cav'ern		cen'tred	
cav'il		cen'tring	
cav'ity		cen'tury	
cease		ceram'ics	
ceased		ce'real	
cease'less		ceremo'nial	
cease'lessly		ceremo'nious	
ceas'ing		cer'emony	
ce'dar		cer'tain	
cede		cer'tainly	
ce'ded		cer'tainty	
ceil'ing		cert'ifiable	
cel'ebrate		certif'icate	
cel'ebrated		certif'icated	
cel'ebrating		certifica'tion	
celebra'tion		cer'tified	
celeb'rity		cer'tify	
celer'ity		cessa'tion	
cel'ery		chafe	
celes'tial		chafed	
cel'ibacy		chaff	
cel'ibate		cha'fing	
cell		chagrin'	
cel'lar		chain	
cell'ophane		chair	
cel'luloid		chair'man	
cel'lulose		chair'manship	
Celt'ic		chalk	
cement'		chal'lenge	
cement'ed		chal'lenged	
cement'ing		chal'lenger	
cem'etery		cham'ber	
cen'otaph		cham'berlain	
cen'sor		chame'leon	
cen'sorship		champagne'	
cen'sure		cham'pion	
cen'sured		cham'pioned	
cen'suring		cham'pionship	
cen'sus		chance	
cen'suses		chanced	
cent		chan'cellor	
cen'tenary		chan'cery	

change		chat'ted	
change'able		chat'tel	
changed		chat'ter	
chan'ging		chauf'feur	
chan'nel		cheap	
chant		cheap'en	
chant'ed		cheap'ly	
cha'os		cheat	
chaot'ic		cheat'ed	
chap		cheat'ing	
chap'el		check	
chap'eron		check'ing	
chap'lain		check'-up	
chap'ter		cheek	
char		cheer	
char'acter		cheered	
characterist'ic		cheer'ful	
characteris'tic-		cheer'fulness	
ally		cheer'ing	
char'coal		cheer'less	
charge		cheese	
charge'able		chef	
charged		chem'ical	
charg'ing		chem'ist	
char'itable		chem'istry	
char'ity		cheque	
char'la'dy		cheque'-book	
char'latan		cher'ish	
charm		cher'ished	
charm'ing		cher'ry	
charred		cher'ub	
chart		chess	
char'ter		chest	
char'tered		chest'nut	
char'woman		chew	
cha'ry		chewed	
chase		chew'ing	
chased		chic	
chasm		chick'en	
chas'sis		chic'ory	
chaste		chief	
chastise'		chief'ly	
chastised'		chil'blain	
chas'tisement		child	
chastis'ing		child'hood	
chas'tity		child'ish	
chat		child'ishly	
		chil'dren	

chill	Christ'mas
chilled	chromat'ic
chime	chrome
chimed	chro'mium
chim'ney	chrom'osome
chimpan'zee	chron'ic
chin	chron'icle
chi'na	chronolog'-ical
Chinese'	
chintz	chrysan'the-mum
chip	
chirop'odist	chum
chirop'ody	church
	church'yard
chiroprac'tor	churl'ish
chirp	churl'ishly
chis'el	churn
chis'el(l)er	chute
chiv'alrous	chut'ney
chiv'alry	ci'der
chlor'inate	cigar'
chlo'roform	cigarette'
	cinch
choc'olate	cin'der
choice	cin'e
choi'cest	cine-cam'era
choir	cin'ema
choke	cinemat'o-graph
chol'era	
choose	cin'namon
choos'ing	ci'pher
chop	cir'ca
chopped	cir'cle
chop'per	cir'cuit
chop'ping	cir'cuited
cho'ral	circu'itous
chord	cir'cular
chore	
choreog'rapher	cir'cularize
choreog'raphy	
cho'rus	cir'culate
chose	cir'culated
chos'en	cir'culating
Christ	circula'tion
chris'ten	circum'ference
Chris'tendom	circumscribe'
chris'tened	circumscribed'
Chris'tian	cir'cumspect
Christian'ity	

circumspec'-
  tion
cir'cumstance
cir'cumstanced
circumstan'tial
circumvent'
cir'cus
cis'tern
cit'adel
cita'tion
cite
ci'ted
cit'izen
cit'izenship
cit'rus
cit'y
civ'ic
civ'il
civil'ian
civil'ity
civiliza'tion
civ'ilize
civ'ilized
clad
claim
claim'ant
claimed
claim'ing
clam'ber
clam'bered
clam'our,
  clam'or
clam'orous
clamp
clandes'tine
clang
clanged
clap
clar'ify
clash
clashed
clasp
class
classed
clas'sic
clas'sical
classifica'tion
classifi'able

clas'sify
class'room
clat'ter
clause
claustrophob'ia
claw
clawed
clay
clean
cleaned
clean'er
clean'est
clean'ing
clean'liness
clean'ly, adj.
clean'ly, adv.
cleanse
cleans'er
cleans'ing
clear
clear'ance
cleared
clear'er
clear'est
clear'ing
clear'ing-house
clear'ly
clear'ness
clear'-sighted
clear'way
clem'ency
clench
clench'ing
cler'gy
cler'gyman
cler'ic
cler'ical
clerk
clerk'ship
clev'er
clew
cliché
click
cli'ent
clientele'
cliff
cli'mate

climat'ic		clus'ter	
cli'max		clus'tered	
climb		clus'tering	
climbed		clutch	
climb'er		clutch'ing	
climb'ing		coach	
clinch		coach'ing	
cling		coach'work	
cling'ing		coal	
clin'ic		coal'face	
clinic'ian		coal'-gas	
clink		coali'tion	
clink'er		coal'-tar	
clip		coarse	
clipped		coars'en	
clip'ping		coarse'ness	
clique		coars'est	
cloak		coast	
clock		coast'al	
clock'work		coast'guard	
clog		coast'ing	
clogged		coast'line	
clois'ter		coat	
close		coat'ed	
closed		coax	
close'ly		coax'ial	
clos'est		cob'bler	
clos'et		co'caine	
close'up		cock	
clo'sure		co'co	
clot		co'coa	
cloth		cocoon'	
clothe		cod	
cloth'ier		code	
cloth'ing		cod'icil	
cloud		cod'ify	
cloud'burst		co'ed'	
cloud'ed		coeduca'tional	
clo'ver		coerce'	
clo'verleaf		coer'cion	
clown		cof'fee	
club		cof'fer	
club'-house		cof'fin	
clue		cog	
clump		co'gency	
clum'sily		co'gent	
clum'sy		co'gently	
clung			

cog'itate	collide'
cogita'tion	colli'ded
co'gnac	colli'ding
cohere'	col'lier
coher'ence	col'liery
coher'ency	colli'sion
coher'ent	collo'quial
cohe'sion	collo'quialism
cohe'sive	collu'sion
coiffeuse'	co'lon
coiffure'	col'onel
coif'fured	colo'nial
coil	col'onist
coin	coloniza'tion
coin'age	col'onize
coincide'	col'ony
coin'cidence	col'or, col'our
coke	col'ored,
cold	col'oured
cold'er	col'ourful
cold'est	col'oring,
cold'hearted	col'ouring
	colos'sal
cold'ly	colt
cold'ness	Colum'bian
collab'orate	col'umn
collabora'tion	col'umnist
collab'orator	comb
collage'	com'bat
collapse'	com'batant
collapsed'	combed
collaps'ible	combina'tion
col'lar	combine'
col'lared	combin'ing
collate'	combus'tible
colla'ted	combus'tion
collat'eral	come
	come'dian
col'league	com'edy
col'lect, *n.*	comely
collect', *v.*	com'et
collect'ed	com'fort
collec'tion	com'fortable
collect'ive	com'forted
collect'ively	com'forter
collect'or	com'forting
col'lege	com'ic
colle'giate	com'ical

com'ing

command'

command'ed

command'er

command'-
ment

commem'orate

commem'-
orated

commemora'-
tion

commence'

commenced'

commence'-
ment

commend'

commend'able

commenda'-
tion

commen'-
datory

commend'ed

commen'surate

com'ment

com'mentary

com'mented

com'merce

commer'cial

commer'cialize

commer'cially

commissar'

commissa'riat

commis'sion

commis'sioner

commit'

commit'ment

commit'ted

commit'tee

commit'ting

commo'dious

commod'ity

com'mon

com'moner

com'monest

com'monly

com'monplace

com'mon-
wealth

commo'tion

com'mune, *n.*
commune', *v.*

commu'nicate

commu'ni-
cated

communica'-
tion

commun'ion

commu'niqué

com'munism

com'munist

commu'nity

commuta'tion

commute'

com'pact, *n.*
compact', *v., adj.*

compan'ion

compan'ion-
ship

com'pany

com'parable

compar'ative

compar'atively

compare'

compared'

compar'ing

compar'ison

compart'ment

com'pass

compas'sion

compas'sionate

compatibil'ity

compat'ible

compat'riot

compel'

compelled'

compen'dium

com'pensate

com'pensated

com'pensating

compensa'tion

compete'

compet'ed

com'petence

com'petent

com'petently

compet'ing

competi'tion

compet'itive

compet'itor

compila'tion

compile'

compiled'

compi'ler

compla'cency

compla'cent

compla'cently

complain'

complain'ant

complained'

complain'ing

complaint'

complais'ant

com'plement

complement'-
ary

complete'

comple'ted

complete'ly

complete'ness

complet'ing

comple'tion

com'plex

complex'ion

complex'ity

compli'ance

compli'ant

com'plicate

com'plicated

complica'tion

complic'ity

complied'

com'pliment

compliment'-
ary

com'plimented

comply'

comply'ing

compo'nent

compose'

composed'

compo'ser

com'posite

composi'tion

compos'itor

compo'sure

com'pound,
  n.
compound',
  v.

compound'ed

comprehend'

comprehend'ed

comprehend'-
ing

comprehen'-
sible

comprehen'-
sion

comprehen'-
sive

com'press, n.
compress', v.

compressed'

compres'sion

comprise'

comprised'

com'promise

com'promised

comptrol'ler

compul'sion

compul'sorily

compul'sory

compunc'tion

computa'tion

compute'

compu'ter

com'rade

con'cave

conceal'

concealed'

conceal'ment

concede'

conce'ded

conceit'

conceit'ed

conceiv'able

conceive'

conceived'

con'centrate

con'centrated

con'centrating

concentra'tion

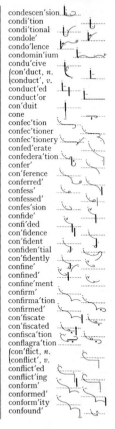

conception'
concern'
concerned'
concerning'
(con'cert, *n.*
(concert', *v.*

concer'to

conces'sion
concession(n)aire'
concil'iate
concil'iated
concilia'tion
concise'
concise'ly
concise'ness
conclude'
conclu'ded
conclu'ding
conclu'sion
conclu'sive
conclu'sively
concoct'
concoct'ed
concoct'ing
concoc'tion
concom'itant
con'cord
con'course
con'crete
concur'
concurred'
concur'rence
concur'rent
concur'rently
concus'sion
condemn'
condemna'tion
condemned'
condemn'ing
condensa'tion
condense'
condensed'
condens'er
condens'ing
condescend'
condescend'ed
condescend'ing

condescen'sion
condi'tion
condi'tional
condole'
condo'lence
condomin'ium
condu'cive
(con'duct, *n.*
(conduct', *v.*
conduct'ed
conduct'or
con'duit
cone
confec'tion
confec'tioner
confec'tionery
confed'erate
confedera'tion
confer'
con'ference
conferred'
confess'
confessed'
confes'sion
confide'
confi'ded
con'fidence
con'fident
confiden'tial
con'fidently
confine'
confined'
confine'ment
confirm'
confirma'tion
confirmed'
con'fiscate
con'fiscated
confisca'tion
conflagra'tion
(con'flict, *n.*
(conflict', *v.*
conflict'ed
conflict'ing
conform'
conformed'
conform'ity
confound'

confound'ed	conscien'-
confront'	tiously
confront'ed	con'scious
confront'ing	con'sciously
confuse'	con'sciousness
confused'	(con'script,
confu'sion	adj.
congeal'	(conscript', v.
conge'nial	conscrip'tion
congen'ially	con'secrate
congen'ital	con'secrated
conges'tion	consecra'tion
conglomera'-	consec'utive
tion	consec'utively
congrat'ulate	consen'sus
congrat'ulated	consent'
congratula'tion	consent'ed
con'gregate	con'sequence
con'gregated	con'sequent
con'gregating	con'sequently
congrega'tion	conserva'tion
congrega'-	conserv'ative
tional	conserv'atively
con'gress	conserve'
congres'sional	consid'er
con'gressmen	consid'erable
conjec'ture	consid'erably
conjec'tured	consid'erate
con'jugal	consid'erately
conjunc'tion	considera'tion
conjure'	consid'ered
con'jure	consid'ering
conjured'	consign'
con'jured	consigned'
con'jurer	consignee'
connect'	consign'er
connect'ed	consign'ment
connec'tion,	consignor'
connex'ion	consist'
conni'vance	consist'ed
connive'	consist'ency
con'quer	consist'ent
con'quered	consist'ently
con'queror	consist'ing
con'quest	consola'tion
con'science	console'
conscien'tious	consoled'
	consol'idate

consol'idated
consol'idating
consolida'tion
con'sonant
consonan'tal
con'sort, *n.*
consort', *v.*
consort'ed
consor'tium
conspic'uous
conspic'uously
conspir'acy
conspir'ator
conspire'
conspired'
con'stable
constab'ulary
con'stant
con'stantly
consterna'tion
constit'uency
constit'uent
con'stitute
con'stituted
con'stituting
constitu'tion
constitu'tional
constitu'tion-
  ally
constrain'
constraint'
constrict'
constrict'ed
constric'tion
construct'
construct'ed
construc'tion
construct'ive
construct'ively
con'strue
con'strued
con'sul
con'sular
consult'
consult'ant
consulta'tion
consult'ed
consult'ing

consume'
consumed'
consu'mer
consum'mate
consumma'-
  tion
consump'tion
consump'tive
con'tact
conta'gion
conta'gious
contain'
contained'
contain'er
contam'inate
contam'inated
contam'inat-
  ing
contamina'-
  tion
con'template
con'templated
con'templating
contempla'tion
contempora'-
  neous
contem'porary
contempt'
contempt'ible
contemp'tuous
contemp'tu-
  ously
contend'
contend'ed
contend'er
con'tent,
  content'
content'ed
content'edly
conten'tion
content'ment
con'tents,
  contents'
{con'test, *n.*
{contest', *v.*
contest'ant
contest'ed
contest'ing

con'text	control'
contig'uous	control'lable
con'tinent	controlled'
continen'tal	control'ler
contin'gency	control'ling
contin'gent	controver'sial
contin'gently	con'troversy
contin'ual	con'trovert
contin'ually	conun'drum
contin'uance	conurba'tion
continua'tion	convales'cence
contin'ue	convales'cent
contin'ued	convec'tor
contin'uing	convene'
continu'ity	convened'
contin'uous	conve'nience
contin'uously	conve'nient
contin'uum	conve'niently
con'tour	con'vent
con'tra	conven'tion
con'traband	conven'tional
contracep'tion	con'versant
contracep'tive	conversa'tion
con'tract, n.	conversa'tional
contract', v.	con'verse, n., adj.
contract'ed	converse', v.
contrac'tion	conversed'
contract'or	con'versely
contradict'	conver'sion
contradict'ed	con'vert, n.
contradic'tion	convert', v.
contradict'ory	convert'ed
contrap'tion	convert'ible
con'trary	con'vex
con'trast, n.	convey'
contrast', v.	convey'ance
contrast'ed	convey'or
contrast'ing	con'vict, n.
contravene'	convict', v.
contraven'tion	convict'ed
contrib'ute	convict'ing
contrib'uted	convic'tion
contrib'uting	convince'
contribu'tion	convinced'
contrib'utor	convin'cing
contrib'utory	conviv'ial
contri'vance	
contrive'	

(con'voy, *n.*	
(convoy', *v.*	
convulse'	
convul'sion	
convul'sive	
cook	
cooked	
cook'er	
cook'ery	
cook'ing	
cool	
cool'ant	
cooled	
cool'er	
cool'est	
coo'lie	
cool'ly	
co-op'erate	
co-op'erated	
co-op'erating	
co-opera'tion	
co-op'erative	
co-op'erator	
co-opt'	
co-or'dinate, *v.*	
co-or'dinate, *n.a.*	
co-ordina'tion	
co-ord'inator	
copart'nership	
cope	
cop'ied	
co'-pi'lot	
co'ping	
co'pious	
cop'per	
cop'y	
cop'yholder	
cop'ying	
cop'yright	
cop'y-wri'ter	
cor'al	
cord	
cor'dial	
cordial'ity	
cor'don	
cor'duroy	
core	
cork	

cork'screw	
corn	
cor'ner	
cor'nice	
corol'lary	
corona'tion	
cor'oner	
cor'porate	
corpora'tion	
corps	
corpse	
cor'pulence	
cor'pulency	
cor'pulent	
cor'puscle	
correct'	
correct'ed	
correct'ing	
correc'tion	
correct'ive	
correct'ly	
correct'ness	
cor'relate	
cor'related	
correla'tion	
correspond'	
correspond'ed	
correspond'- ence	
correspond'ent	
correspond'ing	
cor'ridor	
corrob'orate	
corrob'orated	
corrob'orating	
corrobora'tion	
corrob'orative	
corrob'oratory	
corrode'	
corro'ded	
corro'sion	
corro'sive	
corrupt'	
corrup'tion	
cort'isone	
co'sily	

cosmet′ic	count′ess
cos′monaut	count′ing
cosmop′olis	count′ing-
cosmopol′itan	house
cost	count′less
cost′liness	count′ry
cost′ly	
cos′tume	count′ryman
co′sy	coun′tryside
co′terie	count′y
cot′tage	coupé′
cot′ton	coup′le
couch	cou′pon
cough	cour′age
coughed	coura′geous
cough′ing	course
could	coursed
coun′cil	court
coun′cillor,	court′eous
coun′cilor	court′esy
coun′sel	court-mar′tial
coun′selled,	cous′in
coun′seled	couture′
coun′sellor,	couturier′
coun′selor	
count	cov′enant
count′ed	cov′er
coun′tenance	cov′er-charge
count′er	cov′ered
counteract′	cov′ering
counteract′ed	cov′et
counter-	cov′etous
bal′ance	cow
counter-	cow′ard
bal′anced	cow′ardice
counterbal′-	coy
ancing	co′zily
coun′terblast	co′zy
count′erclaim	crab
	crack
count′erfeit	cracked
count′erfeited	cra′dle
count′erfeiter	craft
count′erfoil	craft′ily
countermand′	craft′iness
counter-	crafts′man
mand′ed	craft′y
count′erpart	cram
	cramp

cramped	
cran'berry	
crane	
crank	
crash	
crashed	
crash'-landing	
crate	
cra'ter	
crave	
craved	
cra'ving	
crawl	
crawled	
cray'on	
craze	
crazed	
cra'zy	
creak	
creaked	
cream	
crease	
creased	
create'	
crea'ted	
crea'tion	
crea'tive	
creativ'ity	
crea'tor	
crea'ture	
cre'dence	
creden'tial	
credibil'ity	
cred'ible	
cred'it	
cred'itable	
cred'ited	
cred'iting	
cred'itor	
credu'lity	
cred'ulous	
creed	
creek	
creep	
creep'ing	
cre'ole	
crêpe	
crept	

cres'cent	
crest	
cretonne'	
crev'ice	
crew	
crib	
crick'et	
crick'eter	
cried	
crime	
crim'inal	
crim'son	
crip'ple	
cri'sis	
crisp	
crite'rion	
crit'ic	
crit'ical	
crit'icism	
crit'icize	
crit'icized	
cro'chet	
cro'cheted	
crock'ery	
crook	
crook'ed	
crop	
crop'per	
croquette'	
cross	
crossed	
cross-examina'tion	
cross-exam'ine	
cross-exam'ining	
cross'-ref'erence	
cross'roads	
cross'-sec'tion	
cross'word	
crowd	
crowd'ed	
crowd'ing	
crown	
crowned	
cru'cial	

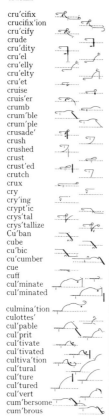

cru'cifix
crucifix'ion
cru'cify
crude
cru'dity
cru'el
cru'elly
cru'elty
cru'et
cruise
cruis'er
crumb
crum'ble
crum'ple
crusade'
crush
crushed
crust
crust'ed
crutch
crux
cry
cry'ing
crypt'ic
crys'tal
crys'tallize
Cu'ban
cube
cu'bic
cu'cumber
cue
cuff
cul'minate
cul'minated
culmina'tion
culottes'
cul'pable
cul'prit
cul'tivate
cul'tivated
cultiva'tion
cul'tural
cul'ture
cul'tured
cul'vert
cum'bersome
cum'brous

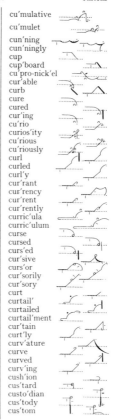

cu'mulative
cu'mulet
cun'ning
cun'ningly
cup
cup'board
cu'pro-nick'el
cur'able
curb
cure
cured
cur'ing
cu'rio
curios'ity
cu'rious
cu'riously
curl
curled
curl'y
cur'rant
cur'rency
cur'rent
cur'rently
curric'ula
curric'ulum
curse
cursed
curs'ed
cur'sive
curs'or
cur'sorily
cur'sory
curt
curtail'
curtailed
curtail'ment
cur'tain
curt'ly
curv'ature
curve
curved
curv'ing
cush'ion
cus'tard
custo'dian
cus'tody
cus'tom

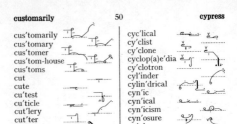

cus'tomarily	cyc'lical
cus'tomary	cy'clist
cus'tomer	cy'clone
cus'tom-house	cyclop(a)e'dia
cus'toms	cy'clotron
cut	cyl'inder
cute	cylin'drical
cu'test	cyn'ic
cu'ticle	cyn'ical
cut'lery	cyn'icism
cut'ter	cyn'osure
cybernet'ics	cy'pher
cy'cle	cy'press

D

dab'ble		dash		
dad		dash'board		
dad'dy		dashed		
dai'ly		das'tardly		
dain'ty		da'ta		
dai'ry		date		
da'is		da'ted		
dai'sy		date'-line		
dam		daugh'ter		
dam'age		daunt		
dam'aged		daunt'ed		
dam'aging		daunt'less		
dam'ask		dav'it		
dame		dawn		
damn		day		
damp		day'break		
damp'en		day'light		
damp'er		day'time		
damp'ness		daze		
dance		daz'zle		
danced		daz'zled		
dan'cer		dead		
dan'cing		dead'beat		
dan'dy		dead'en		
dan'ger		dead'ened		
dan'gerous		dead'lock		
dan'gerously		deaf		
Da'nish		deaf'-aid		
dare		deaf'en		
dared		deaf'ened		
dar'ing		deal		
dar'ingly		deal'er		
dark		dealt		
dark'en		dean		
dark'er		dear		
dar'ling		dear'er		
darn		dear'est		
darned		dearth		
dart		death		
dart'ed		débâc'le		

51

debag'	dec'imal
debar'	dec'imate
debarred'	decima'tion
debar'ring	deci'pher
debase'	deci'phered
debased'	deci'sion
deba'table	deci'sive
debate'	deci'sively
deba'ted	deck
deba'ting	decked
deben'ture	declara'tion
debil'ity	declare'
deb'it	declared'
deb'ited	declar'ing
deb'iting	declen'sion
debonair'	decline'
débris'	decli'ning
debt	decliv'ity
debt'or	declutch'
debunk'	decode'
début'	decompose'
déb'utant	decomposed'
	decomposi'tion
déb'utante	decompress'
	decontam'inate
dec'ade	decontrol'
dec'adence	dec'orate
decay'	dec'orated
decayed'	decora'tion
decay'ing	dec'orative
decease'	dec'orator
deceased'	deco'rous
deceit'	deco'rum
deceit'ful	de'coy
deceit'fulness	decoyed'
deceive'	decoy'ing
decel'erate	decrease'
Decem'ber	decreased'
de'cency	decree'
de'cent	decreed'
de'cently	decrep'it
decentraliza'tion	decried'
decen'tralize	decry'
decep'tion	ded'icate
decep'tive	ded'icated
de'cibel	dedica'tion
decide'	deduce'
deci'ded	deduced'
deci'dedly	

deduct'	
deduct'ed	
deduct'ing	
deduc'tion	
deduct'ive	
deed	
deem	
deemed	
deep	
deep'en	
deep'er	
deep'est	
deep'ly	
deer	
deface'	
defaced'	
deface'ment	
defal'cate	
defalca'tion	
defama'tion	
defam'atory	
defame'	
default'	
default'ed	
default'er	
default'ing	
defeat'	
defeat'ed	
defeat'ing	
defeat'ist	
defect'	
defect'ive	
defence'	
defend	
defend'ant	
defend'ed	
defen'sible	
defen'sive	
defer'	
def'erence	
deferen'tial	
defer'ment	
deferred'	
defer'ring	
defi'ance	
defi'ant	

defi'ciency	
defi'cient	
defi'ciently	
def'icit	
defied'	
define'	
defined'	
def'inite	
def'initely	
defini'tion	
deflate'	
defla'tion	
deflect'	
deflect'ed	
deform'	
deformed'	
deform'ity	
defraud'	
defraud'ed	
defraud'ing	
defray'	
defrayed'	
defray'ing	
de'frost'	
deft	
deft'ly	
defunct'	
defy'	
degen'erate, n. & a.	
de'generate, v.	
degen'erated	
degrada'tion	
degrade'	
degra'ded	
degree'	
dehyd'rate	
deign	
deigned	
de'ity	
deject'	
deject'ed	
dejec'tion	
delay'	
delayed'	
delay'ing	
del'egate, n.	
dele'gate, v.	

del'egated	demoli'tion
del'egating	demonetiza'tion
delega'tion	demon'strate
delete'	demon'strated
delete'rious	demon'strating
dele'tion	demonstra'tion
delib'erate, *adj.*	demon'strative
delib'erate, *v.*	dem'onstrator
delibera'tion	demor'alize
del'icacy	demor'alized
del'icate	demor'alizing
delicatess'en	demo'tion
deli'cious	demur'
delight'	demure'
delight'ed	demur'rage
delight'ful	demurred'
delin'eate	demy'
delinea'tion	deni'al
delin'quency	denied'
delin'quent	de'nim
delir'ious	denom'inating
delir'ium	denomina'tion
deliv'er	denomina'tional
deliv'erance	denote'
deliv'ered	deno'ted
deliv'ering	deno'ting
deliv'ery	denounce'
del'ta-wing	denounced'
delude'	dense
delu'ded	dense'ly
delu'ding	den'sity
del'uge	dent
delu'sion	den'tal
delve	den'tifrice
demand'	den'tist
demand'ed	den'tistry
demand'ing	denuncia'tion
demarca'tion	deny'
demean'our, demean'or	deo'dorize
demerar'a	depart'
demo'bilize	depart'ed
democ'racy	depart'ing
dem'ocrat	depart'ment
democrat'ic	department'al
demol'ish	depar'ture
demol'ished	

depend'	derange'ment
depend'able	der'elict
depend'ed	derelic'tion
depend'ence	deride'
depend'ent	deri'ded
deplete'	deri'sion
deple'ted	deri'sive
deple'ting	deriva'tion
deple'tion	deriv'ative
deplor'able	derive'
deplore'	deri'ving
deplored'	descend'
deplor'ing	descend'ant
deport'	descend'ed
deport'ed	descent'
deport'ment	describe'
depose'	descri'bing
deposed'	descried'
depos'it	descrip'tion
depos'itary	descrip'tions
depos'ited	descrip'tive
depos'iting	descry'
deposi'tion	des'ecrate
depos'itor	desecra'tion
depos'itory	des'ert, n., adj.
dep'ot	desert', v.
depraved'	desert'ed
deprav'ity	desert'er
dep'recate	desert'ing
dep'recated	deser'tion
depre'ciate	deserve'
depre'ciated	deserv'edly
depre'ciating	deserv'ing
deprecia'tion	desidera'tum
depress'	design'
depressed'	des'ignate
depres'sion	des'ignated
depriva'tion	designa'tion
deprive'	designed'
deprived'	design'er
depth	desirabil'ity
deputa'tion	desir'able
depute'	desire'
depu'ted	desired'
depu'ting	desir'ing
dep'utize	desir'ous
dep'uty	desist'
derange'	

desist'ed
desist'ing
desk
des'olate, *adj.*
des'olate, *v.*
desola'tion
despair'
despaired'
despair'ing
despair'ingly
despatch'
despera'do
des'perate
despera'tion
des'picable
despise'
despised'
despite'
despoil'
despoiled'
despoil'er
despond'ency
despond'ent
des'pot
dessert'
destina'tion
des'tine
des'tiny
des'titute
destitu'tion
destroy'
destroy'er
destroy'ing
destruc'tion
destruc'tive
destruc'tively
des'ultory
detach'
detach'ing
detach'ment
de'tail, *n.*
detail', *v.*
detailed'
detain'
detained'
detect'
detect'ed
detec'tion

detec'tive
deten'tion
deter'
dete'riorate
dete'riorated
deteriora'tion
determina'tion
deter'mine
deterred'
deter'rent
deter'ring
detest'
detest'able
detesta'tion
detest'ed
detest'ing
det'onate
det'onated
detona'tion
det'onator
detour'
detract'
detract'ed
detract'or
detrain'
det'riment
detrimen'tal
deval'uate
dev'astate
dev'astated
devasta'tion
devel'op
devel'oped
devel'oping
devel'opment
de'viate
de'viated
devia'tion
devia'tionist
device'
dev'il
de'vious
devise'
devised'
devoid'
devolve'
devolved'

devolv′ing	
devote′	
devo′ted	
devo′tedly	
devotee′	
devo′ting	
devo′tion	
devour′	
devoured′	
devour′ing	
devout′	
dew	
dexter′ity	
dex′terous	
diabe′tes	
diabol′ic	
diagnose′	
diagno′sis	
diag′onal	
di′agram	
di′al	
di′alect	
di′alling,	
di′aling	
di′alogue	
diam′eter	
diamet′ric	
diamet′rical	
di′amond	
di′aphragm	
di′arist	
di′ary	
⎰dic′tate, *n.*	
⎱dictate′, *v.*	
dicta′ted	
dicta′ting	
dicta′tion	
dicta′tor	
dictato′rial	
dicta′torship	
dic′tion	
dic′tionary	
dic′tum	
did	
die	
died	
die′hard	
di′et	

di′etary	
di′eted	
dietet′ics	
di′eting	
dif′fer	
dif′fered	
dif′ference	
dif′ferent	
differen′tiate	
dif′ferently	
dif′ficult	
dif′ficulty	
dif′fidence	
dif′fident	
diffuse′	
diffused′	
diffu′sion	
dig	
di′gest, *n.*	
digest′, *v.*	
digest′ed	
digest′ible	
digest′ing	
diges′tion	
digest′ive	
dig′it	
dig′nify	
dig′nity	
digress′	
digres′sion	
dike	
dilap′idate	
dilap′idated	
dilapida′tion	
dilap′idator	
dilata′tion	
dilate′	
dil′atory	
dilem′ma	
dil′igence	
dil′igent	
dil′igently	
dilute′	
dilu′ted	
dilu′tion	
dim	

dimen'sion	disagree'ing
dimin'ish	disagree'ment
dimin'ished	disallow'
diminu'tion	disappear'
dimin'utive	disappear'ance
dimmed	disappeared'
din	disappear'ing
dine	disappoint'
di'ner	disappoint'ed
din'gey,	disappoint'ing
din'ghy	disappoint'-
din'gy	ment
di'ning	disapproba'-
di'ning-room	tion
din'ner	disapprov'al
dint	disapprove'
di'ocese	disapprov'ing
di'ode	disarm'
dip	disarm'ament
di'phone	disarmed'
diphthe'ria	disarrange'
diph'thong	disarranged'
diplo'ma	disas'ter
diplo'macy	disas'trous
dip'lomat	disas'trously
diplomat'ic	disband'
dire	disband'ed
direct'	disbelief'
direct'ed	disbelieve'
direc'tion	disbelieved'
direct'or	disburse'
direct'orate	disbursed'
direct'ory	disburse'ment
dirn'dl	disc
dirt	discard'
dirt'y	discard'ed
disabil'ity	discard'ing
disa'ble	discern'
disa'blement	discerned'
disa'bling	discern'ible
disadvan'tage	discern'ing
disadvanta'-	discern'ment
geous	discharge'
disadvanta'-	discharged'
geously	discharg'ing
disagree'	disci'ple
disagree'able	disciplina'rian
disagreed'	dis'ciplinary

dis'cipline

disc'-jock'ey

disclaim

disclose'

disclosed'

disclo'sure

discol'our,
discol'or

discol'oured

discom'fit

discom'fited

discom'fiture

discom'fort

disconcert'

disconcert'ed

disconnect'

discontent'

discontent'ed

discontin'ue

discontin'ued

dis'cord

discord'ant

{ dis'count, n.
{ discount', v.

discount'ed

discour'age

discour'age-
ment

discourse

discov'er

discov'ered

discov'ering

discov'ery

discred'it

discred'itable

discred'ited

discreet'

discrep'ancy

discre'tion

discrim'inate,
a.

discrim'inate,
v.

discuss'

discussed'

discus'sion

disdain'

disease'

diseased'

disembark'

disembarka'-
tion

disestab'lish

disestab'-
lished

disestab'lish-
ment

disfa'vour,
disfa'vor

disfig'ure

disfig'urement

disfig'uring

disfran'chise

disgorge'

disgrace'

disgraced'

disgrace'ful

disgrace'fully

disguise'

disguised'

disgust'

disgust'ed

disgust'ing

dish

disheart'en

disheart'ened

disheart'ening

dishev'el

dishev'elled,
dishev'eled

dishon'est

dishon'estly

dishon'esty

dishon'our,
dishon'or

dishon'ourable

dishon'oured

disillu'sion

disincen'tive

disinclina'tion

disinclined'

disinfect'

disinfect'ant

disinfect'ed

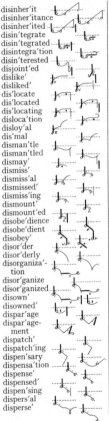

disinher'it
disinher'itance
disinher'ited
disin'tegrate
disin'tegrated
disintegra'tion
disin'terested
disjoint'ed
dislike'
disliked'
dis'locate
dis'located
dis'locating
disloca'tion
disloy'al
dis'mal
disman'tle
disman'tled
dismay'
dismiss'
dismiss'al
dismissed'
dismiss'ing
dismount'
dismount'ed
disobe'dience
disobe'dient
disobey'
disor'der
disor'derly
disorganiza'-
    tion
disor'ganize
disor'ganized
disown'
disowned'
dispar'age
dispar'age-
    ment
dispatch'
dispatch'ing
dispen'sary
dispensa'tion
dispense'
dispensed'
dispen'sing
dispers'al
disperse'

dispersed'
dispers'ing
displace'
displaced'
displace'ment
display'
displayed'
display'ing
displease'
displeased'
displeas'ure
dispo'sal
dispose'
disposed'
disposi'tion
dispossess'
dispossessed'
dispropor'-
    tionate
disprove'
disput'able
dis'putant
dispute'
dispu'ted
dispu'ting
disqualifica'-
    tion
disqual'ify
disqual'ifying
disregard'
disregard'ed
disrep'utable
disrepute'
disrespect'
disrespect'ful
disrup'tion
dis'satisfac'tion
dissat'isfied
dissect'
dissec'tion
dissent'
dissent'ed
dissim'ilar
dis'sipate
dis'sipated
dissipa'tion
dissolu'tion
dissolve'

dissuade'
dissua'ded
dis'tance
dis'tant
dis'tantly
distaste'
distaste'ful
distem'per
distil', distill'
distilled'
distil'lery
distinct'
distinc'tion
distinct'ive
distinct'ively
distinct'ly
distin'guish
distin'guish-
  able
distin'guished
distin'guishing
distort'
distort'ed
distor'tion
distract'
distract'ed
distrac'tion
distrain'
distress'
distressed'
distress'ful
distrib'ute
distrib'uted
distrib'uter
distrib'uting
distribu'tion
distrib'utor
dis'trict
distrust'
distrust'ed
distrust'ful
disturb'
disturb'ance
disturbed'
disturb'ing
disuse', n.
disuse', v.
disused'

ditch
dit'to
divan'
dive
di'ver
diverge'
diver'gent
di'vers
diverse'
diver'sified
diver'sion
diver'sity
divert'
divert'ed
divide'
divi'ded
div'idend
divi'ding
divine'
divine'ly
divin'ity
divis'ible
divi'sion
divi'sional
divorce'
divorced'
divorcee'
divulge'
diz'zy
do
do'cile
dock
docker
dock'et
dock'yard
doc'tor
doc'trine
doc'ument
documen'tary
dod'derer
dodge
does, *v.*
dog
dog'ma
dogmat'ic
do'ing
dole
dole'ful

doll	down'cast
dol'lar	down'fall
domain'	down'hearted
dome	down'hill
domes'tic	down'pour
domes'ticate	down'right
domes'ticated	down'stairs
dom'icile	down'wards
dom'inant	doze
dom'inate	dozed
dom'inated	doz'en
domina'tion	drab
domineer'ing	drachm
Domin'ican	draft
domin'ion	draft'ed
donate'	drag
dona'ted	drain
dona'ting	drain'age
dona'tion	drake
done	dram
do'nor	dra'ma
doo'dle	dramat'ic
doom	dram'atist
door	drank
door'step	drape
door'way	dra'per
dope	dras'tic
dor'mant	dras'tically
dor'mitory	draught
dose	draughts'man
dot	draught'y
dot'ted	draw
dot'ting	drawee'
doub'le	draw'er
doubt	draw'ing
doubt'ed	drawl
doubt'ful	drawn
doubt'fully	dray
doubt'ing	dread
doubt'ingly	dread'ed
doubt'less	dread'ful
doubts	dread'ing
douche	dread'nought
dough	dream
dough'nut	dreamed
dove'tail	dreamt'
dove'tailed	drear'y
down	dredge

dredg'er		dubi'ety	
dregs		du'bious	
drench		du'cal	
Dres'den		duch'ess	
dress		duch'y	
dress'er		duck	
dress'maker		duc'tile	
dried		due	
dri'er		du'el	
drift		duet'	
drift'ed		dug	
drift'ing		duke	
drill		dull	
drilled		du'ly	
drink		dumb	
drink'er		dumbfound'	
drip		dumbfound'ed	
drive		dump	
driv'el		dun	
driv'en		dunce	
dri'ver		dune	
dri'ving		dun'ning	
driz'zle		duoden'al	
drom'edary		dupe	
drone		du'plex	
droop		du'plicate,	
drop		*n. & a.*	
dross		du'plicate, *v.*	
drought		du'plicated	
drouth		duplica'tion	
drove		du'plicator	
drown			
drow'siness		duplic'ity	
drow'sy		durabil'ity	
drudge		du'rable	
drudg'ery		dural'umin	
drug		dura'tion	
drug'gist		dur'ing	
drum		dusk	
drum'mer		dusk'y	
drunk		dust	
drunk'ard		dust'ed	
drunk'en		dust'er	
drunk'enness		Dutch	
dry		du'tiable	
dry'clean		du'tiful	
dry'-rot		du'ty	
du'al		dwarf	

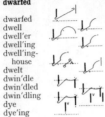

dwarfed	dy'er
dwell	dy'ing
dwell'er	dynam'ic
dwell'ing	dy'namite
dwell'ing-	dy'namo
house	dy'namotor
dwelt	dy'nasty
dwin'dle	dysenter'ic
dwin'dled	dys'entery
dwin'dling	dyspep'sia
dye	dyspep'tic
dye'ing	dyspros'ium

E

educa'tionist		el'derly	
ed'ucator		el'dest	
eel		elect'	
ee'rie, ee'ry		elect'ed	
efface'		elec'tion	
efface'ment		elect'or	
effect'		elect'oral	
effect'ed		elect'orate	
effect'ing		elec'tric	
effect'ive		elec'trical	
effect'ively		elec'trically	
effects'		electri'cian	
effec'tual		electric'ity	
effem'inate		electrifica'tion	
effervesce'		elec'trified	
efferves'cent		elec'trify	
effica'cious		elec'trocute	
ef'ficacy		elec'trocuted	
effi'ciency		electrol'ysis	
effi'cient		elec'tron	
ef'fort		electron'ic	
ef'fortless		electron'ics	
egg		el'egance	
Egyp'tian		el'egant	
eh		el'egantly	
ei'derdown		el'ement	
eight		elemen'tary	
eighteen		el'ephant	
eighteenth		el'evate	
eighth		el'evated	
eight'ieth		eleva'tion	
eight'y		el'evator	
ei'ther		elev'en	
ejac'ulate		elev'enth	
ejac'ulated		elic'it	
ejacula'tion		elic'ited	
eject'		eligibil'ity	
eject'ed		el'igible	
ejec'tion		elim'inate	
elab'orate, adj.		elim'inated	
elab'orate, v.		elim'inating	
elab'orately		elimina'tion	
elabora'tion		Elizabe'than	
elapse'		elm	
elas'tic		elocu'tion	
elastic'ity		elocu'tionist	
el'bow		e'longate	
el'der		e'longated	

elonga'tion		embroca'tion	
elope'		embroid'er	
elope'ment		embroid'ery	
el'oquence		em'bryo	
el'oquent		emend'	
el'oquently		emenda'tion	
else		em'erald	
else'where		emerge'	
elu'cidate		emer'gency	
elu'cidated		em'ery	
elucida'tion		emet'ic	
elude'		em'igrant	
elu'sive		em'igrate	
elu'sively		em'igrated	
ema'ciate		emigra'tion	
ema'ciated		em'inence	
em'anate		em'inent	
em'anating		em'inently	
eman'cipate		em'issary	
emancipa'tion		emis'sion	
embalm'		emit'	
embalmed'		emol'ument	
embank'ment		emo'tion	
embar'go		emo'tional	
embark'		em'pathy	
embarka'tion		em'peror	
embar'rass		em'phasis	
embar'rass-ment		em'phasize	
em'bassy		em'phasized	
embed'		emphat'ic	
embed'ded		emphat'ically	
embel'lish		em'pire	
embel'lish-ment		empir'ical	
embez'zle		employ'	
embez'zled		employ'able	
embez'zle-ment		employee'	
embez'zler		employees'	
embit'ter		employ'er	
em'blem		employ'ing	
embod'ied		employ'ment	
embod'iment		empo'rium	
embod'y		empow'er	
emboss'		empow'ered	
embrace'		em'press	
		emp'tied	
		emp'ty	
		emp'tying	
		em'ulate	

emula'tion	
emul'sion	
ena'ble	
ena'bled	
ena'bling	
enact'	
enact'ed	
enact'ment	
enam'el	
enam'elled, enam'eled	
enam'our, enam'or	
enam'oured	
encamp'	
encamped'	
encamp'ment	
encase'	
encased'	
encash'ment	
enchant'	
enchant'ed	
enchant'ment	
encir'cle	
enclose'	
enclosed'	
enclo'sure	
encoun'ter	
encoun'tered	
encount'ering	
encour'age	
encour'age-ment	
encour'aging	
encroach'	
encroached'	
encroach'ing	
encroach'ment	
encrust'	
encrust'ed	
encum'ber	
encum'bered	
encum'brance	
encyclope'dia	
end	
endan'ger	
endan'gering	
endear	

endeav'our, endeav'or	
end'ed	
end'less	
end'lessly	
endorse'	
endorse'ment	
endow'	
endowed'	
endow'ment	
endur'able	
endur'ance	
endure'	
endured'	
en'emy	
energet'ic	
en'ergy	
en'ervate	
en'ervated	
enfold'	
enfold'ed	
enfold'ing	
enforce'	
enforced'	
enforce'ment	
enforc'ing	
enfran'chise	
enfran'chise-ment	
engage'	
engage'ment	
engen'der	
engen'dered	
en'gine	
engineer'	
engineered'	
engineer'ing	
Eng'lish	
Eng'lishman	
Eng'lishwoman	
engrave'	
engraved'	
engra'ver	
engra'ving	
engross'	
engrossed'	
enhance'	
enhanced'	

enhance′ment

enhan′cing

enig′ma

enigmat′ic

enjoin′

enjoy′

enjoy′able

enjoy′ment

enlarge′

enlarged′

enlarge′ment

enlar′ger

enlar′ging

enlight′en

enlight′ened

enlight′enment

enlist′

enlist′ed

enlist′ing

enlist′ment

enli′ven

enli′vened

en′mity

enor′mity

enor′mous

enough′

enquire′

enquired′

enquir′y

enrage′

enrich′

enrol′, enroll′

enrolled′

enrol′ment

enshrine′

en′sign

ensue′

ensued′

ensu′ing

ensure′

entail′

entailed′

entan′gle

entan′gled

entan′glement

en′ter

en′tered

en′terprise

entertain′

entertained′

entertain′er

entertain′ment

enthuse′

enthu′siasm

enthu′siast

enthusias′tic

enthusias′tic-
ally

entice′

enticed′

entice′ment

entire′

entire′ly

entire′ty

enti′tle

enti′tled

enti′tling

(en′trance, *n.*

(entrance′, *v.*

entranced′

entranc′ing

en′trant

entreat′

entreat′ed

entreat′y

entrust′

entrust′ed

entrust′ing

en′try

enu′merate

enu′merated

enumera′tion

enun′ciate

enun′ciated

enuncia′tion

envel′op

en′velope

en′viable

en′vied

en′vious

envi′ronment

envis′age

en′voy

en′vy

en′zyme

ep′ic

epicen'tre	erra'ta
epidem'ic	errat'ic
ep'ilogue	erra'tum
epis'copal	erred
ep'isode	err'ing
epis'tle	erro'neous
ep'itaph	erro'neously
ep'ithet	er'ror
epit'ome	erst'while
ep'och	er'udite
e'quable	erudi'tion
e'qual	erup'tion
equalitar'ian	es'calator
equal'ity	escape'
equaliza'tion	eschew'
e'qualize	eschewed'
e'qualized	(es'cort, _n._
e'qualled,	(escort', _v._
e'qualed	escort'ed
e'qualling,	espe'cial
e'qualing	espe'cially
e'qually	espy'
equa'tor	esquire'
eq'uerry	es'say
eques'trian	essayed'
equilib'rium	es'sayist
e'quine	es'sence
equip'	essen'tial
equip'ment	estab'lish
equipped'	estab'lished
eq'uitable	estab'lishing
eq'uity	estab'lishment
equiv'alent	estate'
equiv'ocal	esteem'
e'ra	esteemed'
erad'icate	es'timable
erase'	es'timate, _n._
era'ser	es'timate, _v._
era'sure	es'timated
ere	estima'tion
erect'	estrange'
erec'tion	estrange'ment
ergonom'ics	es'tuary
er'mine	et cet'era, etc.
erode'	etch
ero'sion	etch'er
err	etch'ing
er'rand	eter'nal

eter′nity	
e′ther	
ethe′real	
eth′ical	
eth′ics	
eth′yl	
et′iquette	
etymolog′ical	
etymol′ogy	
Euclid	
eugen′ic	
eu′logy	
euphor′ia	
Europe′an	
evac′uate	
evacua′tion	
evade′	
eval′uate	
evalua′tion	
evan′gelist	
evap′orate	
evap′orated	
evapora′tion	
eva′sion	
eva′sive	
eve	
e′ven	
eve′ning	
e′venly	
e′vensong	
event′	
event′ful	
even′tual	
eventual′ity	
even′tually	
ev′er	
everlast′ing	
everlast′ingly	
ev′ery	
ev′erybody	
ev′erything	
everywhere	
evict′	
evic′tion	
ev′idence	
ev′ident	
ev′idently	
e′vil	

evince′	
evoke′	
evoked′	
evolu′tion	
evolve′	
ewe	
ew′er	
exact′	
exact′ly	
exag′gerate	
exaggera′tion	
exalt′	
exalt′ed	
exalta′tion	
examina′tion	
exam′ine	
exam′iner	
exam′ining	
exam′ple	
exas′perate	
exas′perated	
exaspera′tion	
ex′cavate	
ex′cavated	
excava′tion	
exceed′	
exeeed′ingly	
excel′	
excelled′	
ex′cellence	
ex′cellent	
ex′cellently	
excel′sior	
except′	
except′ed	
except′ing	
excep′tion	
excep′tional	
ex′cerpt	
excess′	
excess′ive	
excess′ively	
exchange′	
exchanged′	
exchang′ing	
excise′	
excite′	
excite′ment	

exclaim′	exhort′ed
exclaimed′	ex′igency
exclama′tion	ex′ile
exclude′	ex′iled
exclu′sion	exist′
exclu′sive	exist′ed
exclu′sively	exist′ence
excru′ciate	exist′ent
excur′sion	existen′tial
excu′sable	exist′ing
{excuse′, *n.*	ex′it
{excuse′, *v.*	exor′bitant
excused′	expand′
ex′ecute	expand′ed
ex′ecuted	expanse′
execu′tion	expan′sion
exec′utive	expan′sionist
exec′utor	expan′sive
exec′utrix	
exem′plary	expect′
exem′plify	expect′ed
exempt′	expect′ant
exemp′tion	expect′antly
ex′ercise	expecta′tion
ex′ercised	expect′ing
exert′	expe′diency
exert′ed	expe′dient
exer′tion	expe′diently
exhale′	ex′pedite
exhaled′	ex′pedited
exha′ling	expedi′tion
exhaust′	expel′
exhaust′ed	expelled′
exhaust′ing	expend′
exhaustion	expend′ed
exhaust′ive	expend′iture
exhaust′ively	expense′
exhib′it	expen′sive
exhib′ited	expen′sively
exhib′iting	expe′rience
exhibi′tion	expe′riencing
exhibi′tionist	exper′iment
exhib′itor	experimen′tal
exhil′arate	ex′pert
exhil′arated	expertise′
exhilara′tion	expira′tion
exhort′	expire′
exhorta′tion	expired′

expi'ry		extinc'tion	
explain'		extin'guish	
explained'		extin'guished	
explana'tion		extin'guisher	
explan'atory		extol'	
explic'it		extolled'	
explode'		extor'tion	
explo'ded		ex'tra	
exploit'		ex'tract, n.	
exploita'tion		extract', v.	
explora'tion		extract'ed	
explore'		extrac'tion	
explored'		ex'tradite	
explor'er		ex'tradited	
explo'sion		ex'traditing	
explo'sive		extradi'tion	
expo'nent		extra'neous	
ex'port, n.		extraor'din-	
export', v.		arily	
export'ed		extraor'dinary	
export'er		extrav'agance	
export'ing		extrav'agant	
expose'		extrav'agantly	
exposi'tion			
expo'sure		extreme'	
express'		extrem'ity	
express'ion		ex'tricate	
express'ive		ex'tricated	
express'ly		ex'trovert	
expul'sion		exu'berance	
ex'quisite		exu'berant	
ex'tant		exude'	
extempora'-		exult'	
neous		exulta'tion	
extend'		exult'ed	
extend'ed		eye	
exten'sion		eye'ball	
exten'sive		eye'brow	
extent'		eyed	
exten'uate		eye'ing, ey'ing	
exten'uating		eye'lash	
extenua'tion		eye'lid	
exte'rior		eye'-op'ener	
exter'minate		eyes	
extermina'tion		eye'sight	
		eye'sore	
exter'nal		eye'wash	
extinct'		eye'-witness	

F

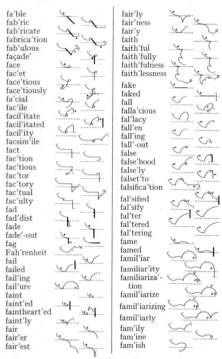

fa'ble
fab'ric
fab'ricate
fabrica'tion
fab'ulous
façade'
face
fac'et
face'tious
face'tiously
fa'cial
fac'ile
facil'itate
facil'itated
facil'ity
facsim'ile
fact
fac'tion
fac'tious
fac'tor
fac'tory
fac'tual
fac'ulty
fad
fad'dist
fade
fade'-out
fag
Fah'renheit
fail
failed
fail'ing
fail'ure
faint
faint'ed
faintheart'ed
faint'ly
fair
fair'er
fair'est

fair'ly
fair'ness
fair'y
faith
faith'ful
faith'fully
faith'fulness
faith'lessness
fake
faked
fall
falla'cious
fal'lacy
fall'en
fall'ing
fall'-out
false
false'hood
false'ly
falset'to
falsifica'tion
fal'sified
fal'sify
fal'ter
fal'tered
fal'tering
fame
famed
famil'iar
familiar'ity
familiariza'-
    tion
famil'iarize
famil'iarizing
famil'iarly
fam'ily
fam'ine
fam'ish

fam′ished	fatal′ity
fam′ishing	fa′tally
fa′mous	fate
fan	fate′ful
fanat′ic	fa′ther
fanat′ical	fa′ther-*in*-law
fanat′icism	fa′therland
fan′cied	fa′therless
fan′ciful	fath′om
fan′cifully	fatigue′
fan′cy	fat′ten
fantas′tic	fatu′ity
fantas′tical	fat′uous
	fault
fantas′tically	fault′less
fan′tasy	fault′y
far	fau′na
farce	fa′vour, fa′vor
far′cical	fa′vourable
fare	fa′voured
fared	fa′vourite
farewell′	fa′vouritism
	fawn
farina′ceous	fear
farm	feared
farmed	fear′ful
farm′er	fear′ing
farm′house	fear′less
far′sighted	feasibil′ity
far′ther	fea′sible
far′thest	fea′sibly
farth′ing	feast
fas′cinate	feast′ing
fascina′tion	feat
fash′ion	feath′er
fash′ionable	feath′ery
fash′ioned	fea′ture
fast	fea′tured
fast′en	fea′tureless
fast′ened	Feb′ruary
fast′ener	fed
fast′er	fed′eral
fast′est	fed′eralism
fastid′ious	fed′eralist
fast′ing	federa′tion
fat	fee
fa′tal	fee′ble
fa′talism	feed
fa′talist	

feed'er	
feed'ing	
feel	
feel'ing	
feel'ingly	
feet	
feign	
feint	
felic'itate	
felic'itated	
felicita'tion	
felic'itous	
felic'ity	
fe'line	
fell	
felled	
fel'low	
fel'lowship	
fel'on	
felo'nious	
felo'niously	
fel'ony	
felt	
fe'male	
fem'inine	
fem'inism	
fence	
fenced	
fen'cer	
fend'er	
{fer'ment, *n.*	
{ferment', *v.*	
fermenta'tion	
ferment'ed	
fern	
fero'cious	
feroc'ity	
ferroconc'rete	
fer'ry	
fer'tile	
fertil'ity	
fertiliza'tion	
fer'tilize	
fer'tilizer	
fer'vent	
fer'vently	
fer'vid	

fer'vour, fer'- vor	
fes'ter	
fes'tered	
fes'tival	
fes'tive	
festiv'ity	
fetch	
fetch'ing	
fet'ter	
fet'tered	
feud	
feu'dal	
feuds	
fe'ver	
fe'verish	
fe'verishly	
few	
few'er	
fiancé, fiancée	
fias'co	
fi'at	
fib	
fi'bre	
fi'breglass	
fibrosit'is	
fi'brous	
fick'le	
fic'tion	
ficti'tious	
fid'dle	
fidel'ity	
fidg'et	
fidg'ety	
fidu'ciary	
field	
fiend	
fiend'ish	
fierce	
fierc'est	
fi'ery	
fi'es'ta	
fifteen'	
fifteenth'	
fifth	
fif'ty	
fig	

fight		fin'ger	
fight'er		fin'gered	
fight'ing		fin'ical	
fig'ment		fi'nis	
fig'urative		fin'ish	
fig'uratively		fin'ished	
fig'ure		fin'ishing	
fig'urehead		fir	
figurine'		fire'arms	
fil'ament		fire'brand	
filch		fire'clay	
file		fire'-damp	
filed		fired	
fil'ial		fire'-engine	
fi'ling		fire'man	
fill		fire'place	
filled		fire'proof	
fill'er		fire'side	
fil'let		fire'wood	
fil'leted			
fill'ing		fire'works	
fill'ip		fir'ing	
film		firm	
fil'ter		fir'mament	
fil'tered		firm'er	
filth			
fil'trate		firm'ly	
filtra'tion		firm'ness	
fin		*first*	
fi'nal		*first*-class	
final'ity		*first*-hand	
fi'nally		*first'ly*	
finance'		*first*-rate	
financed'		firth	
finan'cial		fis'cal	
finan'cially		fish	
finan'cier		fished	
find		fish'er	
find'er		fish'ery	
find'ing		fish'-hook	
fine		fis'sure	
fined		fis'sured	
fine'drawn		fist	
fine'ly		fit	
fi'ner		fit'ful	
fi'nery		fit'ly	
finesse'		fit'ness	
fi'nest			

fit'ted		flaunt'ed	
fit'ter		fla'vour,	
fit'test		fla'vor	
fit'ting		fla'voured	
fit'tingly		fla'vouring	
five		flaw	
fiv'er		flaw'less	
fix		flax	
fixa'tion		flay	
fixed		flea	
fix'edly		fled	
fix'ture		flee	
fiz'zle		fleece	
fiz'zled		fleet	
flab'by		flesh	
flac'cid		flew	
flag		flexibil'ity	
flag'on		flex'ible	
fla'grant		flick	
fla'grantly		flick'er	
flag'-ship		flick'ered	
flake		fli'er	
flaked		flight	
flamboy'ant		flight'y	
flame		flim'sily	
flan		flim'sy	
flange		flinch	
flank		fling	
flan'nel		flint	
flannelette		flip'pancy	
flap		flip'pant	
flap'per		flip'pantly	
flare		flirt	
flared		flirt'ing	
flash		flit	
flashed		flit'ted	
flask		flit'ting	
flat		float	
flat'ly		float'ed	
flat'ten		flock	
flat'tened		flocked	
flat'ter		flog	
flat'tered		flogged	
flat'terer		flood	
flat'tery		flood'ing	
flat'ulence		flood'light	
flat'ulent		floor	
flaunt		floor'ing	

flop		flut'tered	
flo'ral		flux	
flor'id		fly	
flor'in		fly'er	
flor'ist		fly'leaf	
floss		fly'over	
flota'tion		fly'-wheel	
flotil'la		foam	
flot'sam		fob	
flounce		fo'cus	
floun'der		fo'cus(s)ed	
floun'dered		fod'der	
flour		foe	
flour'ish		fog	
flour'ished		fogged	
flour'ishing		fog'gy	
flout		foil	
flout'ed		foiled	
flow		foist	
flowed		fold	
flow'er		fold'ed	
flow'ered		fold'er	
flow'ery		fold'ing	
flow'ing		fo'liage	
flown		fo'lio	
fluc'tuate		folk	
fluc'tuated		folk'lore	
fluc'tuating		fol'low	
fluctua'tion		fol'lowed	
flue		fol'lower	
flu'ency		fol'lowing	
flu'ent		fol'ly	
flu'ently		foment'	
fluff		fomenta'tion	
fluff'y		fond	
flu'id		fond'er	
fluke		fond'est	
flung		fon'dle	
flunk'ey		fon'dled	
fluores'cent		fond'ly	
flur'ried		food	
flur'ry		food'stuff	
flush		fool	
flushed		fooled	
flus'ter		fool'hardy	
flus'tered		fool'ish	
flute		fool'ishly	
flut'ter		fools'cap	

foot	
foot'ball	
foot'board	
foot'hold	
foot'ing	
foot'lights	
foot'mark	
foot'note	
foot'print	
foot'sore	
foot'step	
foot'stool	
for	
for'age	
for'ay	
forbad', for-	
bade'	
(for'bear, *n.*	
(forbear', *v.*	
forbear'ance	
forbid'	
forbid'den	
force	
forced	
force'ful	
for'ceps	
for'cible	
ford	
ford'ed	
fore	
fore'arm	
forebo'ding	
(fore'cast, *n.*	
(forecast', *v.*	
foreclose'	
foreclo'sure	
fore'court	
fore'father	
forego'	
forego'ing	
foregone'	
fore'ground	
fore'hand	
fore'head	
for'eign	
for'eigner	
fore'man	
fore'most	

fore'noon	
forerun'ner	
foresee'	
foresee'able	
foreseen'	
foreshad'ow	
fore'sight	
for'est	
forestall'	
forestalled'	
for'ester	
for'estry	
foretell'	
fore'thought	
foretold'	
forev'er	
forewarn'	
forewarned'	
fore'word	
for'feit	
for'feited	
for'feiture	
forgave'	
forge	
for'ger	
for'gery	
forget'	
forget'ful	
forget'fulness	
forgive'	
forgive'ness	
forgiv'ing	
forgo'	
forgot'	
forgot'ten	
fork	
forlorn'	
form	
form'al	
formal'ity	
forma'tion	
formed	
for'mer	
for'merly	
for'midable	
for'mula	
for'mulate	
forsake'	

forsa'ken	fox
forsook'	fracas
fort	frac'tion
forth	frac'tious
forth'coming	frac'ture
forth'right	frac'tured
forthwith'	frag'ile
for'tieth	fragil'ity
fortifica'tion	frag'ment
for'tified	frag'mentary
for'tify	fra'grance
for'titude	fra'grant
fort'night	frail
fort'nightly	frail'ty
for'tress	frame
fortu'itous	framed
for'tunate	fra'mer
for'tunately	frame'work
for'tune	franc
for'ty	fran'chise
fo'rum	fran'chisement
	frank
for'ward	frank'ly
for'warding	frank'ness
for'wards	fran'tic
fos'sil	frater'nal
fos'ter	frater'nity
fos'tered	fraud
fos'tering	fraud'ulent
fought	fraud'ulently
foul	fraught
fouled	fray
foul'ly	frayed
found	freak
founda'tion	freck'le
found'ed	free
foun'der	freed
foun'dered	free'dom
foun'dry	free'hold
fount	free'lance
foun'tain	free'ly
foun'tain-head	fre'er
four	freeze
four'some	freez'ing
fourteen'	freight
fourteenth'	freight'age
fourth	freight'ed
fowl	

French	
French'man	
fren'zied	
fren'zy	
fre'quency	
fre'quent, *adj.*	
frequent', *v.*	
frequent'ed	
frequent'ing	
fre'quently	
fres'co	
fresh	
fresh'en	
fresh'ened	
fresh'ening	
fresh'er	
fresh'est	
fresh'ly	
fret	
fret'ful	
fret'ted	
fret'ting	
fri'ar	
fric'tion	
Fri'day	
fried	
friend	
friend'less	
friend'lier	
friend'liest	
friend'liness	
friend'ly	
friend'ship	
frieze	
fright	
fright'en	
fright'ful	
fright'fulness	
frig'id	
frigid'ity	
frill	
frilled	
fringe	
frisk	
frit'ter	
frit'tered	
frivol'ity	
friv'olous	

friv'olously	
frock	
frog	
frol'ic	
from	
front	
front'age	
fron'tal	
fron'tier	
fron'tispiece	
frost	
frost'bite	
frost'ed	
frost'y	
froth	
frown	
frowned	
frown'ing	
froze	
fro'zen	
fru'gal	
frugal'ity	
fruit	
fruit'ful	
fruit'fulness	
frui'tion	
fruit'less	
fruit'lessness	
frus'trate	
frus'trated	
frustra'tion	
fry	
fuch'sia	
fudge	
fu'el	
fu'gitive	
fulfil'	
fulfilled'	
fulfil'ment	
full	
full'est	
full'-length	
full'ness	
full'y	
ful'some	
fum'ble	
fum'bled	
fume	

fumed		fur'rier	
fu'migate		fur'row	
fu'migated		fur'rowed	
fumiga'tion		fur'ther	
fun		fur'therance	
func'tion		fur'thered	
func'tioned		fur'thermore	
fund		fur'thermost	
fundamen'tal		fur'thest	
		fur'tive	
fu'neral		fur'tively	
fune'real		fu'ry	
fun'gus		fuse	
fun'nel		fused	
fun'niest		fu'selage	
fun'ny		fu'sible	
fur		fusillade'	
fu'rious		fu'sion	
fu'riously		fuss	
furl		fuss'y	
furled		fust'y	
fur'long		fu'tile	
fur'lough		futil'ity	
fur'nace		fu'ture	
fur'nish		fu'turist	
fur'nisher		futuris'tic	
fur'niture		futu'rity	

G

gab'erdine
ga'ble
Gael'ic
gadg'et
gaffe
gag
gage
gagged
gai'ety, gay'ety
gai'ly, gay'ly
gain
gained
gain'ing
gait
ga'la
gale
gall
gal'lant,
  gallant'
gal'lantry
gal'lery
gal'lon
gal'lop
galore'
galvan'ic
gal'vanize

gal'vanized

gam'ble
gam'bler
gam'bling
gam'bol
game
ga'mut
gan'der
gang
gang'ster
gang'way
gaol
gaol'er

gap
gape
garage
garb
gar'bage
gar'den
gar'dener
gar'gle
gar'land
gar'ment
gar'ner
gar'nered
gar'nish
garnishee'
gar'ret
gar'rison
gar'rulous
gar'ter
gas
gash
gashed
gas'-meter
gas'olene
gasom'eter
gasp
gas'tric
gate
gâ'teau
gath'er
gath'ered
gath'ering
gauge
gaunt
gaunt'let
gauze
gave
gay
gay'est
gaze

gazed		geriat'ric	
gazette'		germ	
gazetteer'		Ger'man	
gear		germane'	
geared		gestic'ulate	
geese		gestic'ulated	
gel'atine		ges'ture	
gem		get	
gen'der		get'ting	
gen'eral		gey'ser	
general'ity		ghast'ly	
generaliza'tion		ghost	
gen'eralize		gi'ant	
gen'eralized		gibe	
gen'erally		gid'dy	
gen'erate		gift	
gen'erated		gift'ed	
gen'erating		gigan'tic	
genera'tion		gild	
gen'erator		gild'ed	
generosity		gill (of a fish)	
gen'erous		gill (a measure)	
gen'erously		gilt	
gen'esis		gimm'ick	
ge'nial		gin	
genial'ity		gin'ger	
ge'nius		gip'sy, gyp'sy	
gen'ocide		gird	
genteel'		gird'ed	
Gen'tile		gird'er	
gen'tle		gir'dle	
gen'tleman		girl	
gen'tlemanly		girl'hood	
gen'tlemen		girth	
gen'tleness		gist	
gen'tly		give	
gen'uine		giv'en	
gen'uinely		giv'er	
geograph'ic		gives	
geograph'ical		giv'ing	
geog'raphy		glacé	
geolog'ical		gla'cial	
geol'ogist		glac'ier	
geol'ogy		glad	
geomet'ric		glad'den	
geomet'rical		glade	
geomet'rically		glad'ly	
geom'etry		glad'ness	

glam'orous		glut'ton	
glam'our,		glut'tonous	
glam'or		glyc'erine	
glance		gnash	
glanced		gnaw	
glan'cing		gnawed	
gland		go	
glare		goad	
glared		go'-ahead	
glass		goal	
glass'ful		goat	
glass'ware		gob'ble	
glass'y		gob'let	
glaze		God	
glazed		god'ly	
gleam		go'ing	
gleamed		gold	
glean		gold'en	
gleaned		gold'smith	
glee		golf	
glen		golf'er	
glib		golosh'	
glide		gone	
glim'mer		gong	
glimpse		good	
glint		good-bye'	
glis'ten		good-	
glis'tened		hu'moured	
glit'ter		goodna'ture	
glit'tered		goodna'tured	
global		good'ness	
globe		good-night'	
gloom		goods	
gloom'y		good'-sized	
glorifica'tion		goodwill'	
glo'rify		goose	
glo'rious		gore	
glo'ry		gored	
gloss		gorge	
glos'sary		gorged	
gloss'y		gor'geous	
glove		goril'la	
glow		gos'pel	
glu'cose		gos'sip	
glue		got	
glu'ey		Goth'ic	
glum		gouge	
glut			

gov'ern	
gov'erned	
gov'erning	
gov'ernment	
governmen'tal	
gov'ernor	
gov'ernorship	
gown	
grab	
grace	
grace'ful	
grace'fully	
gra'cious	
gra'ciously	
grada'tion	
grade	
gra'ded	
gra'dient	
gra'ding	
grad'ual	
grad'ually	
grad'uate	
grad'uated	
gradua'tion	
graffi'ti	
graft	
graft'ed	
graft'er	
graft'ing	
grain	
gram'mar	
gramma'rian	
grammat'ical	
gram'ophone	
gran'ary	
grand	
grand'- daughter	
grand'est	
gran'deur	
grand'father	
grand'mother	
grand'parent	
grand'son	
grange	
gran'ite	
grant	
grant'ed	

gran'ulate	
gran'ulated	
grape	
graph'ic	
graph'ically	
graph'ite	
grap'ple	
grap'pled	
grap'pling	
grasp	
grasped	
grasp'ing	
grass	
grass'y	
grate	
grate'ful	
gratifica'tion	
grat'ified	
grat'ify	
gra'tis	
grat'itude	
gratu'itous	
gratu'ity	
grave	
grav'el	
grave'ly	
gravita'tion	
grav'ity	
gra'vy	
gray, grey	
graze	
grazed	
grease	
greas'y	
great	
great'er	
great'est	
great'ly	
great'ness	
Gre'cian	
greed	
greed'ily	
greed'y	
Greek	
green	
green'house	
greet	

greet'ed	grow'er
greet'ing	growl
grega'rious	growled
grew	grown
grey'hound	growth
grid	grub
grief	grudge
griev'ance	grudg'ingly
grieve	grue'some
grieved	gruff
griev'ous	gruff'ly
griev'ously	grum'ble
grill, grille	grum'bled
grilled	grunt
grim	grun'ted
grimace'	guarantee'
grime	guaranteed'
grin	guarantee'ing
grinned	guarantor'
grin'ning	guaranty
grind	guard
grind'er	guard'ed
grind'ing	guard'ian
grip	guard'ianship
gripe	guard'ing
grit	guess
groan	guessed
groaned	guess'work
groan'ing	guest
gro'cer	guid'ance
gro'cery	guide
groom	guild
groove	guild'hall
grooved	guile
grope	guillotine'
gross	guilt
grotesque'	guilt'y
ground	guin'ea
ground'less	guise
ground'-nut	guitar'
ground'-plan	gulf
ground'work	gull
group	gulled
grouped	gul'let
group'ing	gul'lible
grove	gulp
grov'el	gum
grow	gummed

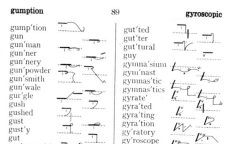

gump'tion
gun
gun'man
gun'ner
gun'nery
gun'powder
gun'smith
gun'wale
gur'gle
gush
gushed
gust
gust'y
gut
gut'ta-per'cha

gut'ted
gut'ter
gut'tural
guy
gymna'sium
gym'nast
gymnas'tic
gymnas'tics
gyrate'
gyra'ted
gyra'ting
gyra'tion
gy'ratory
gy'roscope
gyroscop'ic

H

hab'it
hab'itable
habita'tion
habit'ual
habit'uate
hack
hack'ney
hack'neyed
had
haem'orrhage,
  hem'orrhage
hag
hag'gard
hag'gle
hail
hailed
hair
hair'dresser
hair'y
hale
half
half'-caste
half-heart'ed
half-nelson
half'-price
hall
hall'mark
hal'low
halt
halt'ed
hal'ter
halve
halved
ham
ham'hand'ed
ham'let
ham'mer
ham'mered
ham'mock
ham'per

ham'pered
hand
hand'bag
hand'ed
hand'ful
hand'icap
hand'icraft
hand'ing
hand'iwork
hand'kerchief
hand'le
hand'led
hand'ling
hand'-made
hand'out
hand'some

hand'work
hand'writing
hand'y
hang
hang'ar
hanged
hang'er
hang'over
hank'er
haphaz'ard
hap'pen
hap'pened
hap'pening
hap'pier
hap'piest
hap'pily
hap'piness
hap'py
harangue'
harangued'
har'ass
har'bour,
  har'bor

90

hard		haugh'ty	
hard'board		haul	
hard'en		haul'age	
hard'ened		hauled	
hard'er		haunt	
hard'est		haunt'ed	
hard'-hearted		Havan'a	
hard'ly		*have*	
hard'ness		ha'ven	
hard'ship		*hav'ing*	
hard'ware		hav'oc	
hard'y		hawk	
hare		hawk'er	
harm		haw'thorn	
harmed		hay	
harm'ful		hay'stack	
harm'less		haz'ard	
harmon'ics		haz'ardous	
harmo'nious		haze	
har'monize		ha'zel	
har'mony		ha'ziness	
har'ness		ha'zy	
harp		he	
harpoon'		head	
har'row		head'ache	
har'rowed		head'light	
har'rowing		head'line	
harsh		head'long	
harsh'ly		headmast'er	
har'vest		head'quart'ers	
har'vested		head'stone	
har'vesting		head'strong	
has		head'way	
hash		heal	
haste		healed	
ha'sten		health	
ha'stened		health'ful	
ha'stily		health'ier	
ha'sty		health'iest	
hat		health'y	
hatch		heap	
hatched		hear	
hatch'et		heard	
hatch'ing		hear'er	
hate		hear'ing	
hate'ful		hear'say	
hate'fully		heart	
ha'tred			

heart'en	hen
heart'ening	hence
heart'felt	henceforth'
hearth	
heart'ily	hencefor'ward
heart'y	
heat	her
heat'ed	her'ald
heat'er	her'alded
heath	her'aldry
heath'en	herb
heat'ing	Hercu'lean
heave	herd
heav'en	herd'ed
heav'enly	here
heav'ily	hereaf'ter
heav'y	hereby'
Hebra'ic	hered'itary
He'brew	hered'ity
heck'le	herein'
hec'tic	hereof'
hedge	hereon'
heed	hereto'
heed'ful	heretofore'
heed'less	hereun'der
heel	herewith'
heif'er	her'itage
height	her'mit
height'en	he'ro
hei'nous	hero'ic
heir	he'roin
heir'ess	her'oine
held	her'oism
hel'icopter	her'ring
hel'iport	hers
hell	herself'
helm	hes'itancy
helm'et	hes'itant
help	hes'itate
help'er	hes'itated
help'ful	hes'itating
help'fulness	hes'itatingly
help'less	hesita'tion
help'lessness	hew
hem	hewed
hem'isphere	hewn
hemp	hex'agon
hemp'en	hia'tus
	hid

hid'den		
hide		
hid'eous		
hi'ding		
hieroglyph'ic		
hi'fi		
high		
high'brow		
high'er		
high'est		
high-hand'ed		
high'land		
high'ly		
high'ness		
high'road		
high'way		
hi'-jacker		
hike		
hi'ker		
hila'rious		
hilar'ity		
hill		
hill'side		
hilt		
him		
himself'		
hin'der		
hin'dered		
hin'dering		
hin'drance		
Hin'du		
hinge		
hint		
hint'ed		
hint'ing		
hip		
hire		
hired		
hire'-pur'chase		
hir'ing		
his		
hiss		
hissed		
hist'amine		
histo'rian		
histor'ic		
histor'ical		
his'tory		

hit		
hitch		
hith'er		
hither*to'*		
hive		
hoard		
hoard'ed		
hoard'er		
hoard'ing		
hoarse		
hoarse'ly		
hoarse'ness		
hoax		
hoaxed		
hob'ble		
hob'by		
hock'ey		
hod		
hoe		
hoed		
hoes		
hog		
hoist		
hoist'ed		
hoist'ing		
hold		
hold'er		
hold'ing		
hold'up		
hole		
hol'iday		
ho'liness		
hol'low		
hol'lowed		
ho'ly		
hom'age		
home		
home'coming		
home'less		
home'ly		
home'sick		
home'stead		
home'ward		
home'work		
hom'icide		
hom'ily		
homoge'neous		
hom'onym		

hon′est		host	
hon′estly		hos′tage	
hon′esty		hos′tel	
hon′ey		host′ess	
hon′eymoon		hos′tile	
honora′rium		hostil′ity	
hon′orary		hot	
hon′our,		hotel′	
hon′or		hot′house	
hon′ourable		hot′ter	
hon′oured		hot′test	
hon′ours		hound	
hood		*hour*	
hood′wink		*hour′ly*	
hoof		house	
hook		house′hold	
hop		house′holder	
hope		house′keeper	
hope′ful		house′keeping	
hope′fulness		house′work	
hope′less		hous′ing	
hope′lessness		hov′el	
hop′ing		hov′er	
horde		hov′ering	
hori′zon		*how*	
horizon′tal		howev′er	
hor′mone		howl	
horn		howled	
hor′rible		howsoev′er	
hor′rid		hub	
hor′rified		hud′dle	
hor′rify		hue	
hor′ror		huff	
hors-d'oeuv′res		hug	
horse		huge	
horse′back		hulk	
Horse′ Guards		hull	
horse′hair		hum	
horse′man		hu′man	
horse′manship		humane′	
horse′-power		humane′ly	
		humanis′tic	
hort′iculture		humanita′rian	
		human′ity	
hose		hu′manly	
ho′siery		hum′ble	
hos′pitable		hum′bler	
hos′pital		hum′blest	
hospital′ity			

hum'bly		hus'band	
hum'bug		hus'banded	
hu'mid		hus'banding	
humid'ity		hush	
humil'iate		hushed	
humil'iated		husk	
humilia'tion		husk'ily	
humil'ity		husk'iness	
hummed		husk'y	
hu'morist		hus'tle	
hu'morous		hus'tled	
hu'mour,		hus'tler	
hu'mor		hut	
hu'moured		hy'brid	
hump		hy'drant	
hunch		hydraul'ic	
hun'dred		hy'drofoil	
hun'dredth		hy'drogen	
hun'dred-		hy'drophone	
weight		hydropon'ics	
hung		hy'giene	
Hunga'rian		hygien'ic	
hun'ger		hymn	
hun'gered		hyper'bole	
hun'ger-strike		hypercrit'ical	
hun'gry		hyperson'ic	
hunt		hy'phen	
hunt'ed		hypnos'is	
hunt'er		hyp'notism	
hunt'ing		hyp'notize	
hunts'man		hypoc'risy	
hur'dle		hyp'ocrite	
hurl		hypocrit'ical	
hurled		hypothet'ical	
hurrah'		hysterec'tomy	
hur'ricane		hyste'ria	
hur'ried		hyster'ical	
hur'ry		hyster'ics	
hurt		hythe	
hurt'ful			

I

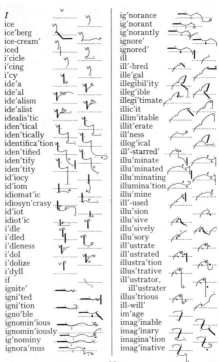

I

ice
ice'berg
ice-cream'
iced
i'cicle
i'cing
i'cy
ide'a
ide'al
ide'alism
ide'alist
idealis'tic
iden'tical
iden'tically
identifica'tion
iden'tified
iden'tify
iden'tity
id'iocy
id'iom
idiomat'ic
idiosyn'crasy
id'iot
idiot'ic
i'dle
i'dled
i'dleness
i'dol
i'dolize
i'dyll
if
ignite'
igni'ted
igni'tion
igno'ble
ignomin'ious
ignomin'iously
ig'nominy
ignora'mus

ig'norance
ig'norant
ig'norantly
ignore'
ignored'
ill
ill'-bred
ille'gal
illegibil'ity
illeg'ible
illegi'timate
illic'it
illim'itable
illit'erate
ill'ness
illog'ical
ill'-starred'
illu'minate
illu'minated
illu'minating
illumina'tion
illu'mine
ill'-used
illu'sion
illu'sive
illu'sively
illu'sory
ill'ustrate
ill'ustrated
illustra'tion
illus'trative
ill'ustrator,
    ill'ustrater
illus'trious
ill-will'
im'age
imag'inable
imag'inary
imagina'tion
imag'inative

96

imag'ine		im'pact, *n.*	
imag'ined		impact', *v.*	
imag'ining		impair'	
im'becile		impaired'	
imbecil'ity		impart'	
imbibe'		impart'ed	
imbibed'		impar'tial	
imbue'		impartial'ity	
imbued'		impas'sable	
im'itate		impas'sioned	
im'itated		impas'sive	
im'itating		impa'tience	
imita'tion		impa'tient	
im'itative		impa'tiently	
im'itator		impeach'	
immac'ulate		impeach'ment	
immate'rial		impecu'nious	
immature'		impede'	
immeas'urable		imped'iment	
imme'diate		impel'	
imme'diately		impelled'	
immemo'rial		impend'	
immense'		impend'ing	
immense'ly		impen'etrable	
immen'sity		impen'itent	
immerse'		imper'ative	
immer'sion		imper'atively	
im'migrant		impercep'tible	
im'migrate		imper'fect	
immigra'tion		imperfec'tion	
im'minence		imper'fectly	
im'minent			
immo'bile		imper'il	
immod'erate		impe'rious	
immod'erately		imper'ishable	
immod'est		imper'sonal	
immod'estly		imper'sonate	
immor'al		impersona'tion	
immoral'ity		imper'tinence	
		imper'tinent	
immor'tal		imper'tinently	
immortal'ity		imperturb'able	
immor'talize		imper'vious	
		impet'uous	
immov'able		impet'uously	
immune'		im'petus	
immu'nity		impinge'	
immu'table		im'pious	
imp			

impla'cable
implant'
implant'ed
implement
im'plicate
implica'tion
implic'it
implied'
implore'
implored'
imply'
impolite'
{im'port, n.
{import', v.
impor'tance
impor'tant
importa'tion
import'ed
import'er
impor'tunate
importune'
impose'
imposi'tion
impossibil'ity
impos'sible
im'post
impos'tor
impos'ture
im'potence
im'potency
im'potent
im'potently
impound'
impound'ed
impov'erish
impov'erished
impov'erish-
    ment
imprac'tic-
    able
impreca'tion
impreg'nable
{im'press, n.
{impress', v.
impres'sion
impres'sion-
    able
impress'ive

impress'ively
{im'print, n.
{imprint', v.
imprint'ed
impris'on
impris'oned
impris'onment
improbabil'-
    ity
improb'able
improb'ably
impromp'tu
improp'er
improp'erly
impropri'ety
improve'
improved'
improve'-
    ment
improv'idence
improv'ident
improv'idently
improv'ing
improviza'tion
improvize'
impru'dence
impru'dent
impru'dently
im'pudence
im'pudent
im'pudently
impugn'
impugned'
im'pulse
impul'sive
impul'sively
impu'nity
impure'
impu'rity
imputa'tion
impute'
impu'ted
impu'ting
in
inabil'ity
inaccess'ible
inac'curacy
inac'curate

inac'curately	
inac'tion	
inact'ive	
inactiv'ity	
inad'equacy	
inad'equate	
inadmis'sible	
inadvert'ent	
inadvert'ently	
inane'	
inan'imate	
inani'tion	
inan'ity	
inappro'priate	
inapt'	
inapt'itude	
inartic'ulate	
inartis'tic	
inasmuch'	
inatten'tion	
inatten'tive	
inaud'ible	
inau'gural	
inau'gurate	
inaugura'tion	
inauspi'cious	
inauspi'ciously	
in'born	
in'bred	
incal'culable	
incandes'cence	
incandes'cent	
incapabil'ity	
inca'pable	
incapac'itate	
incapac'itated	
incapac'itating	
incapac'ity	
incar'cerate	
incau'tious	
incau'tiously	
incen'diarism	
incen'diary	
in'cense	
incen'tive	
incep'tion	
inces'sant	

inces'santly	
inch	
in'cidence	
in'cident	
inciden'tal	
incin'erate	
incin'erator	
incip'ient	
inci'sion	
inci'sive	
incite'	
incite'ment	
incivil'ity	
inclem'ency	
inclem'ent	
inclina'tion	
incline'	
inclined'	
inclose'	
inclo'sure	
include'	
inclu'ded	
inclu'ding	
inclu'sion	
inclu'sive	
incoher'ency	
incoher'ent	
in'come	
in'coming	
incom'parable	
incompati- bil'ity	
incompat'ible	
incom'petence	
incom'petent	
incom'petently	
incomplete'	
incomprehen'- sible	
inconceiv'able	
inconclu'sive	
inconclu'sively	
incongru'ity	
incon'gruous	
incon'sequent	
inconsequen'- tial	
inconsid'erable	

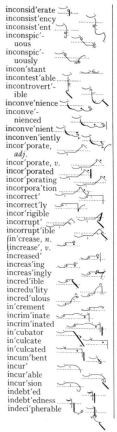

inconsid'erate
inconsist'ency
inconsist'ent
inconspic'-
 uous
inconspic'-
 uously
incon'stant
incontest'able
incontrovert'-
 ible
inconve'nience
inconve'-
 nienced
inconve'nient
inconven'iently
incor'porate,
 adj.
incor'porate, v.
incor'porated
incor'porating
incorpora'tion
incorrect'
incorrect'ly
incor'rigible
incorrupt'
incorrupt'ible
{in'crease, n.
{increase', v.
increased'
increas'ing
increas'ingly
incred'ible
incredu'lity
incred'ulous
in'crement
incrim'inate
incrim'inated
in'cubator
in'culcate
in'culcated
incum'bent
incur'
incur'able
incur'sion
indebt'ed
indebt'edness
indeci'pherable

indeci'sion
indeci'sive
indeed'
indefat'igable
indefen'sible
indefin'able
indef'inite
indel'ible
indel'icacy
indel'icate
indem'nify
indem'nity
indent'
indenta'tion
inden'ture
independ'-
 ence
independ'ent
independ'-
 ently
indescri'bable
indeter'minate
in'dex
in'dexed
In'dian
in'dicate
in'dicated
indica'tion
indic'ative
in'dicator
ind'ices
indict'
indict'able
indict'ment
indif'ference
indif'ferent
indif'ferently
in'digent
indigest'ible
indiges'tion
indig'nant
indig'nantly
indigna'tion
indig'nity
indirect'
indirect'ly

indiscreet'	
indiscre'tion	
indiscrim'inate	
indiscrim'in- ately	
indispen'- sable	
indispen'- sably	
indispose'	
indisposed'	
indisposi'tion	
indispu'table	
indistinct'	
indistin'guish- able	
indite'	
individ'ual	
individ'ualist	
individual'ity	
individ'ually	
indivis'ible	
in'dolence	
in'dolent	
in'dolently	
indom'itable	
in'door	
indorse'	
indorse'ment	
indors'er	
indu'bitable	
induce'	
induced'	
induce'ment	
induct'	
induc'tion	
indulge'	
indul'gence	
indul'gent	
indul'gently	
indul'ging	
indus'trial	
indus'trialist	
industrial- iza'tion	
indus'trious	
in'dustry	
inebria'tion	

ined'ible	
ineffec'tual	
ineffi'ciency	
ineffi'cient	
ineffi'ciently	
inel'egant	
inel'igible	
inequal'ity	
inerad'icable	
inert'	
iner'tia	
ines'timable	
inev'itable	
inexact'	
inexcus'able	
inexhaust'ible	
inex'orable	
inexpe'dient	
inexpen'sive	
inexpe'rience	
inex'plicable	
inex'tricable	
infallibil'ity	
infal'lible	
in'famous	
in'famy	
in'fancy	
in'fant	
in'fantile	
in'fantry	
infat'uate	
infatua'tion	
infect'	
infected'	
infec'tion	
infec'tious	
infer'	
in'ference	
infe'rior	
inferior'ity	
infer'nal	
infer'no	
inferred'	
infest'	
infest'ed	
in'fidel	

infidel'ity	infu'riated
in'finite	infuse'
in'finitely	infused'
infinites'imal	inge'nious
	inge'niously
infin'ity	ingenu'ity
infirm'	ingen'uous
infir'mary	ingen'uously
infir'mity	inglo'rious
inflame'	in'got
inflamed'	ingrain'
inflammabil'-	in'grate
ity	ingra'tiate
inflam'mable	ingra'tiated
inflamma'tion	ingra'tiating
inflate'	ingrat'itude
infla'ted	ingre'dient
infla'ting	inhab'it
infla'tion	inhab'itable
inflec'tion	inhab'itant
inflex'ion	inhab'ited
inflexibil'ity	inhala'tion
inflex'ible	inhale'
inflict'	inhaled'
inflict'ed	inher'ent
inflic'tion	inher'it
in'fluence	inher'itance
in'fluenced	inher'ited
in'fluencing	inhibi'tion
influen'tial	inhos'pitable
influen'tially	inhu'man
influen'za	inim'ical
in'flux	inim'itable
inform'	iniq'uitous
inform'al	iniq'uity
informal'ity	ini'tial
inform'ant	ini'tialled,
informa'tion	ini'tialed
inform'ative	ini'tiate
informed'	ini'tiated
inform'er	initia'tion
inform'ing	ini'tiative
infra'-red	inject'
infre'quent	inject'ed
infre'quently	injec'tion
infringe'	injudi'cious
infringe'ment	injudi'ciously
infu'riate	injunc'tion

in'jure	
in'jured	
inju'rious	
inju'riously	
in'jury	
injus'tice	
ink	
inlaid	
in'land	
in'let	
in'mate	
in'most	
inn	
innate'	
in'ner	
in'nermost	
in'nocence	
in'nocent	
in'nocently	
innoc'uous	
innova'tion	
innuen'do	
innu'merable	
inoc'ulate	
inoc'ulated	
inocula'tion	
inopportune'	
inopportune'ly	
inor'dinate	
inorgan'ic	
in'-patient	
in'put	
in'quest	
inquire'	
inquired'	
inquir'er	
inquir'y	
inquis'itive	
inquis'itively	
in'road	
insane'	
insan'itary	
insan'ity	
insa'tiable	
inscribe'	
inscribed'	
inscri'bing	
inscrip'tion	

inscru'table	
in'sect	
insecure'	
insecu'rity	
insensibil'ity	
insen'sible	
insen'sibly	
insep'arable	
insert'	
insert'ed	
inser'tion	
{in'set, n.	
{inset', v.	
in'side	
insid'ious	
in'sight	
insig'nia	
insignif'icance	
insignif'icant	
insincere'	
insincere'ly	
insincer'ity	
insin'uate	
insin'uated	
insin'uating	
insinua'tion	
insip'id	
insist'	
insist'ed	
insist'ence	
insist'ent	
insist'ently	
insobri'ety	
in'solence	
in'solent	
in'solently	
insol'uble	
insol'vency	
insolv'ent	
insom'nia	
inspect'	
inspect'ed	
inspect'ing	
inspec'tion	
inspec'tor	
inspira'tion	
inspire'	
inspired'	

inspir'ing	
instabil'ity	
install'	
installa'tion	
installed'	
instal'ment	
in'stance	
in'stanced	
in'stant	
instanta'neous	
instanta'ne- ously	
in'stantly	
instead'	
in'step	
in'stigate	
in'stigated	
in'stigator	
instil', instill'	
in'stinct	
instinc'tive	
instinc'tively	
in'stitute	
in'stituted	
institu'tion	
instruct'	
instruct'ed	
instruc'tion	
instruc'tive	
instruct'or	
in'strument	
instrumen'tal	
insubor'dinate	
insubordina'- tion	
insuf'ferable	
insuffi'ciency	
insuffi'cient	
insuffi'ciently	
in'sular	
in'sulate	
in'sulated	
insula'tion	
in'sulator	
in'sulin	
{in'sult, n. {insult', v.	
insult'ed	

insult'ing	
insu'perable	
insupport'able	
insur'able	
insur'ance	
insure'	
insured'	
insur'gent	
insurmount'- able	
insurrec'tion	
intact'	
intan'gible	
in'tegral	
in'tegrate	
integ'rity	
in'tellect	
intellec'tual	
intel'ligence	
intel'ligent	
intel'ligently	
intelligent'sia	
intel'ligible	
intel'ligibly	
intem'perance	
intem'perate	
intem'perately	
intend'	
intend'ed	
intense'	
intense'ly	
inten'sify	
inten'sity	
inten'sive	
intent'	
inten'tion	
inten'tional	
intent'ly	
inter'	
intercede'	
intercept'	
intercept'ed	
{in'terchange, n. {interchange' v.	

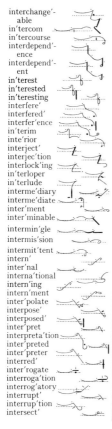

interchange'-
able
in'tercom
in'tercourse
interdepend'-
ence
interdepend'-
ent
in'terest
in'terested
in'teresting
interfere'
interfered'
interfer'ence
in'terim
inte'rior
interject'
interjec'tion
interlock'ing
in'terloper
in'terlude
interme'diary
interme'diate
inter'ment
inter'minable

intermin'gle

intermis'sion

intermit'tent
intern'
inter'nal
interna'tional
intern'ing
intern'ment
inter'polate
interpose'
interposed'
inter'pret
interpreta'tion
inter'preted
inter'preter
interred'
inter'rogate
interroga'tion
interrog'atory
interrupt'
interrup'tion
intersect'

intersect'ed
intersec'tion
intersperse'
interspersed'
intertwine'
in'terval
intervene'
interven'tion
in'terview
interwov'en
intes'tate
intes'tine
in'timacy
in'timate, n.,
   adj.
in'timate, v.
in'timately
in'timating
intima'tion
intim'idate
intim'idated
intimida'tion
in'to

intol'erable
intol'erance
intol'erant
intona'tion
intox'icant
intox'icate
intox'icated
intoxica'tion
intrep'id
in'tricacy
in'tricate
intrigue'
intrin'sic

intrin'sically
introduce'
introduced'
introduc'tion
introduc'tory
introspec'tion
introspec'tive
in'trovert
intrude'
intru'ded
intru'sion

intui'tion	invi'ted
intu'itive	invoca'tion
intu'itively	in'voice
in'undate	in'voiced
in'undated	invoke'
inunda'tion	invoked'
inure'	invol'untary
invade'	involve'
in'valid	involved'
inval'idate	invul'nerable
inval'uable	
inva'riable	in'ward
inva'sion	in'wardly
invec'tive	i'odine
inveigh'	i'onize
invei'gle	ion'osphere
invent'	io'ta
invent'ed	iras'cible
inven'tion	irate'
invent'ive	ire
invent'or	I'rish
in'ventory	irk'some
inverse'	i'ron
inver'sion	iron'ic
invert'	iron'ical
invert'ed	i'ronmonger
invest'	i'rony
invest'ed	irra'tional
inves'tigate	irrecov'erable
inves'tigated	irredeem'able
investiga'tion	
inves'tigator	irredu'cible
invest'ing	irrefu'table
invest'ment	irreg'ular
invest'or	irregular'ity
invet'erate	irrel'evancy
invid'ious	irrel'evant
invigila'tion	irreme'diable
invig'orate	irremov'able
invig'orated	irrep'arable
invin'cible	irrepres'sible
invi'olable	irreproach'able
invi'olate	irresist'ible
invis'ible	irres'olute
invita'tion	irrespec'tive
invite'	irrespec'tively

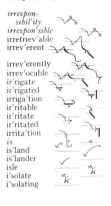

irrespon-	
sibil'ity	
irrespon'sible	
irretriev'able	
irrev'erent	
irrev'erently	
irrev'ocable	
ir'rigate	
ir'rigated	
irriga'tion	
ir'ritable	
ir'ritate	
ir'ritated	
irrita'tion	
is	
is'land	
is'lander	
isle	
i'solate	
i'solating	

isola'tion	
isola'tionist	
is'otope	
is'sue	
is'sued	
is'suing	
it	
Ital'ian	
ital'ic	
ital'ics	
ital'icize	
itch	
i'tem	
i'temize	
itin'erant	
itin'erary	
itin'erate	
its	
itself'	
i'vory	
i'vy	

J

jack			jer'sey	
jack'et			jest	
jack'pot			jest'ed	
Jacobe'an			jest'er	
jade			jest'ing	
ja'ded			jest'ingly	
jag			jet	
jagged			jet'sam	
jag'ged			jet'tison	
jail			jet'ty	
jail'er			Jew	
jail'or			jew'el	
jam			jew'eller,	
jamb			jew'eler	
jammed			jew'ellery	
jan'gle			jew'elry	
jan'gled			Jew'ess	
jan'itor			Jew'ish	
Jan'uary			jibe	
Japan'			jig'saw	
Japanese'			jin'gle	
jar			jitt'ery	
jar'gon			job	
jar'ring			job'ber	
jar'ringly			job'bery	
jaun'dice			jock'ey	
jaunt			jocose'	
jaun'tily			joc'ular	
jaw			jog	
jay'wa'lker			join	
jeal'ous			join'er	
jeal'ousy			join'ing	
jeer			joint	
jeered			joint'ed	
jel'ly			joint'ly	
jeop'ardize			joke	
jeop'ardy			jo'kingly	
jerk			jol'lity	
jerked			jol'ly	
jer'ry			jolt	

108

jos'tle		juice	
jos'tled		juke'-box	
jot		July'	
jot'ted		jum'ble	
jot'ting		jum'bo	
jour'nal		jump	
journalese'		jumped	
jour'nalism		jump'er	
jour'nalist		junc'tion	
journalis'tic		junc'ture	
jour'ney		June	
jour'neyed		jun'gle	
jo'vial		ju'nior	
jovial'ity		junk	
joy		jurisdic'tion	
joy'ful		ju'rist	
joy'ous		ju'ror	
joy'ously		ju'ry	
ju'bilant		ju'ryman	
jubila'tion		just	
ju'bilee		jus'tice	
judge		jus'tifiable	
judged		justifica'tion	
judg'ing		jus'tified	
judg'ment		jus'tify	
ju'dicature		just'ly	
judi'cial		just'ness	
judi'cious		jut	
judi'ciously		jute	
jug		jut'ted	
jug'gle		jut'ting	
jug'gler		ju'venile	
ju'gular		juxtaposi'tion	

K

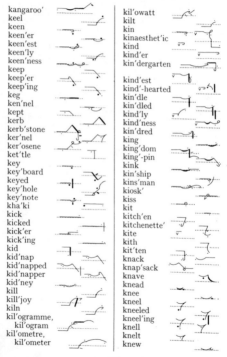

kangaroo'
keel
keen
keen'er
keen'est
keen'ly
keen'ness
keep
keep'er
keep'ing
keg
ken'nel
kept
kerb
kerb'stone
ker'nel
ker'osene
ket'tle
key
key'board
keyed
key'hole
key'note
kha'ki
kick
kicked
kick'er
kick'ing
kid
kid'nap
kid'napped
kid'napper
kid'ney
kill
kill'joy
kiln
kil'ogramme,
  kil'ogram
kil'ometre,
  kil'ometer

kil'owatt
kilt
kin
kinaesthet'ic
kind
kind'er
kin'dergarten
kind'est
kind'-hearted
kin'dle
kin'dled
kind'ly
kind'ness
kin'dred
king
king'dom
king'-pin
kink
kin'ship
kins'man
kiosk'
kiss
kit
kitch'en
kitchenette'
kite
kith
kit'ten
knack
knap'sack
knave
knead
knee
kneel
kneeled
kneel'ing
knell
knelt
knew

110

knife	knot'ting
knight	knot'ty
knight'hood	know
knit	know'-how
knit'wear	know'ing
knives	know'ingly
knob	*knowl'edge*
knock	known
knocked	knuck'le
knock'er	knuck'led
knoll	knuck'ling
knot	ko'dak
knot'ted	ku'dos

L

la'bel
la'belled,
  la'beled
la'belling,
  la'beling
lab'oratory
labo'rious
labo'riously
la'bour, la'bor
la'bourer

labur'num
lab'yrinth
lace
lac'erate
lac'erated
lacera'tion
lach'rymose
la'cing
lack
lackadai'sical
lacked
lacon'ic
lac'quer,
  lack'er
lac'tate
lad
lad'der
la'den
la'dle
la'dy
la'dyship
lag
la'ger
lag'gard
lagged
laid
lain
lair
la'ity

lake
lamb
lam'bent
lame
lamed
lament'
lam'entable
lamenta'tion
lament'ed
lament'ing
lam'ia
lam'inate
lamp
lance
lan'cet
land
land'ed
land'holder
land'ing
land'lady
land'lord
land'mark
land'owner
land'-rover
land'scape
land'slide
lane
lan'guage
lan'guid
lan'guish

lan'gour

lank'y
lan'tern
lap
lapel'
lapse
lapsed
laps'ing
lar'ceny

112

larch	launched	
lard	launch'ing	
lard'er	laun'dry	
large	lau'reate	
large'ly	lau'rel	
larg'er	la'va	
larg'est	lav'atory	
lark	lav'ender	
lar'va	lav'ish	
lar'vae	lav'ished	
laryngi'tis	lav'ishly	
	law	
lar'ynx	law'ful	
	law'fully	
las'car	law'fulness	
la'ser	law'less	
lash	law'lessness	
lashed	lawn	
lash'ing	law'suit	
lass	law'yer	
las'situde	lax	
last	lax'ative	
last'ed	lax'ity	
last'ing	lay	
last'ingly	lay'by	
last'ly	lay'er	
latch	lay'ing	
late	lay'man	
late'ly	lay'out	
la'tent	laze	
la'ter	la'zier	
lat'eral	la'zily	
la'test	la'ziness	
lath	la'zy	
lathe	lea	
lath'er	lead (a metal)	
Lat'in	lead (to con-	
lat'itude	duct)	
lat'ter	lead'en	
lat'terly	lead'er	
lat'tice	lead'ership	
laud	lead'ing	
laud'able	leaf	
laud'anum	leaf'let	
laud'atory	leaf'y	
laugh	league	
laugh'ingly	leagued	
laugh'ter	leak	
launch		

leak'age	le'galize
leak'y	le'gally
lean	legatee'
leaned	lega'tion
lean'est	leg'end
lean'ing	leg'endary
leant	leg'erdemain
leap	legibil'ity
leaped	leg'ible
leap'ing	le'gion
leapt	leg'islate
learn	leg'islated
learned	legisla'tion
learn'ed	leg'islative
learn'er	leg'islator
learn'ing	leg'islature
learnt	legit'imacy
lease	legit'imate, adj.
lease'hold	legitimate', v.
lease'holder	lei'sure
leash	lei'surely
leashed	lem'on
leas'ing	lemonade'
least	lend
leath'er	lend'er
leave	lend'ing
leav'en	length
lec'ture	length'en
lec'tured	length'ening
lec'turer	length'wise
lec'turing	length'y
led	le'nience
ledge	le'niency
ledg'er	le'nient
leek	le'niently
leer	lens
leered	Lent, lent
leer'ing	leop'ard
leer'ingly	lep'er
lee'ward	lep'rosy
	les'bian
lee'way	less
left	lessee'
left'-handed	les'sen
leg	les'sened
leg'acy	les'sening
le'gal	les'ser
legal'ity	

les'son		lick	
lessor'		licked	
lest		lid	
let		lid'o	
le'thal		lie	
lethar'gic		lied	
leth'argy		li'en	
let'ter		lieu	
let'terbox		lieuten'ant	
let'terhead		life	
let'terpress		life'boat	
let'ting		life'guard	
let'tuce		life'-insurance	
leukaem'ia		life'less	
lev'ee		life'-preserver	
lev'el		lifesav'er	
lev'elled, lev'eled		life'-size	
lev'elling, lev'eling		life'time	
le'ver		lift	
le'verage		lift'ed	
levi'athan		lift'ing	
lev'ity		lig'ament	
lev'y		lig'ature	
liabil'ity		light	
li'able		light'ed	
liais'on-officer		light'ening	
li'ar		light'er	
li'bel		light'erage	
li'bellous, li'belous		light'hearted	
lib'eral		light'house	
liberal'ity		light'ing	
lib'erally		light'ning	
lib'erate		like	
lib'erated		like'able	
lib'erating		liked	
libera'tion		like'lihood	
lib'erty		like'ly	
libra'rian		li'ken	
li'brary		li'kened	
{li'cence, n.		like'ness	
{li'cense, v.		like'wise	
li'censed		li'lac	
licensee'		lil'y	
licen'tious		limb	
li'chen		lim'ber	
		lim'bo	
		lime	

lime'light
lime'stone
lime'water
lim'it
limita'tion
lim'ited
lim'iting
lim'ousine
limp
limped
lim'pet
lim'pid
limp'ing
line
lin'eage
lin'eal
lineal'ity
lin'eament
lin'ear
lined
lin'en
li'ner
lin'ger
lin'gered
lin'gerie
lin'guist
linguis'tic
lin'iment
li'ning
link
lino'leum
li'notype
lin'seed
lint
li'on
li'oness
lip
lip'stick
liq'uefy
liqueur'
liq'uid
liq'uidate
liq'uidated
liq'uidating
liquida'tion
liq'uidator
liq'uidize
liq'uor

liq'uorice, lic'orice
lisp
list
list'ed
lis'ten
lis'tened
lis'tener
list'ing
list'less
list'lessly
list'lessness
lit
lit'any
lit'eral
lit'erally
lit'erary
lit'erature
lithe
lithog'rapher
lithograph'ic
lithog'raphy
lit'igant
lit'igate
litiga'tion
lit'ter
lit'tered
lit'tle
lit'urgy
live, v.
live, a.
lived
live'lihood
live'long
live'ly
liv'er
liv'ery
lives
lives, pl.
live'stock
liv'id
load
load'ed
load'ing
loaf
loaf'er
loaf'ing
loam

loan	
loan'ing	
loath, loth	
loathe	
loath'some	
loaves	
lob'by	
lob'ster	
lo'cal	
local'ity	
lo'calize	
lo'cally	
locate'	
loca'ted	
loca'ting	
loca'tion	
loch	
lock	
locked	
lock'er	
lock'et	
lock'out	
lock'smith	
lo'como'tion	
lo'comotive	
lo'cum-te'nens	
lo'cust	
lode	
lodge	
lodged	
lodg'ing	
loft	
loft'ier	
loft'iest	
loft'ily	
loft'y	
log	
log'ic	
log'ical	
logi'cian	
loin	
loi'ter	
loi'tered	
loll	
lolled	
lone	
lone'liness	
lone'ly	

lone'some	
long	
longed	
long'er, n.	
lon'ger, adj.	
lon'gest	
longev'ity	
long'hand	
lon'gitude	
longitu'dinal	
long'lived	
long'suffering	
loo'fah	
look	
looked	
look'ing	
look'out	
loom	
loomed	
loom'ing	
loop	
loop'hole	
loose	
loosed	
loose'ly	
loos'en	
loos'ened	
loos'er	
loqua'cious	
loquac'ity	
lord	
lord'ship	
lore	
lor'ry	
lose	
los'er	
los'ing	
loss	
lost	
lot	
lo'tion	
lot'tery	
loud	
loud'er	
loud'speaker	
lounge	
lov'able	

love	
love'lier	
love'liest	
love'liness	
love'ly	
lov'er	
low	
low'er	
low'ered	
low'est	
low'land	
low'ly	
loy'al	
loy'alty	
loz'enge	
lu'bricant	
lu'bricate	
lu'bricated	
lubrica'tion	
lu'bricator	
lu'cid	
lucid'ity	
luck	
luck'ier	
luck'iest	
luck'y	
lu'crative	
lu'dicrous	
lug'gage	
luke'warm	
lull	
lull'aby	
lulled	

lull'ing	
lumba'go	
lum'ber	
lu'minous	
lump	
lu'nacy	
lu'nar	
lu'natic	
lunch	
lunch'eon	
lung	
lunge	
lurch	
lure	
lured	
lu'rid	
lurk	
lus'cious	
lus'tre	
lus'trous	
lust'y	
lute	
luxu'riance	
luxu'riant	
luxu'rious	
luxu'riously	
lux'ury	
ly'ing	
lynch	
lynx	
lyr'ic	
lyr'ical	

M

maca'bre
macad'amize
mace
machina'tion
machine'
machin'ery
machine'-tool
machin'ist
mack'erel
mack'intosh
macrobiot'ics
mac'ron
mad
mad'am
mad'den
mad'dening
made
maes'tro
magazine'
mag'ic
mag'ical
magi'cian
magiste'rial
mag'istrate
magnanim'ity
magnan'imous
mag'nate
magne'sia
mag'net
magnet'ic
mag'netism
mag'netize
magnet'o
magnif'icence
magnif'icent
magnif'icently
mag'nified

mag'nify
mag'nitude
mahog'any
maid
maid'en
mail
mail'able
mailed
maim
maimed
main
main'land
main'ly
main'spring
main'stay
maintain'
maintain'ed
main'tenance
maize
majes'tic
maj'esty
ma'jor
major'ity
make
ma'ker
make'shift
make'-up
mak'ing
maladjust'ment
mal'ady
mal'aise
mal'aprop
mala'ria
mal'content
male
malev'olent
mal'ice
mali'cious
mali'ciously
malign'

malig'nant	man'ly
maligned'	mann'equin
malin'ger	man'ner
malin'gerer	man'nerly
mal'leable	manoeu'vre
mal'nutri'tion	manoeu'vring
malt	man'-of-war'
maltreat'	man'or
maltreat'ed	man'power
mama',	man'sion
mamma'	man'slaughter
mam'mal	man'tel
mam'moth	man'telpiece
man	mantil'la
man'acle	man'tle
man'age	man'ual
man'agement	*manufac'-*
man'ager	*ture*
man'ageress	*manufac'-*
manage'rial	*tured*
man'date, *n.*	*manufac'turer*
mandate', *v.*	*manufac'turing*
man'datory	manure'
man'dolin	man'uscript
mane	man'y
man'ful	map
man'fully	ma'ple
man'gle	mapped
man'hood	mar
ma'nia	mar'ble
ma'niac	march (March)
mani'acal	marched
man'icure	march'ing
man'ifest	mare
manifesta'tion	mar'gin
man'ifested	mar'ginal
man'ifesting	marine'
man'ifestly	mar'iner
manifes'to	mar'ital
man'ifold	mar'itime
man'ikin	mark
manip'ulate	marked
manip'ulated	mar'ket
	mar'malade
manipula'tion	ma'rocain
mankind'	marred
man'lier	mar'riage

mar'ried	
mar'ring	
mar'row	
mar'ry	
mar'rying	
marsh	
mar'shal	
mar'shalled, mar'shaled	
mart	
mar'tial	
mar'tyr	
mar'tyrdom	
mar'vel	
mar'velled, mar'veled	
mar'vellous, mar'velous	
marx'ist	
mascar'a	
mas'cot	
mas'culine	
mash	
mashed	
mask	
mas'ochism	
mas'ochist	
ma'son	
mason'ic	
ma'sonry	
masquerade'	
Mass, mass	
mas'sacre	
mas'sacred	
massage'	
masseur'	
masseuse'	
mass'ive	
mass'ively	
mast	
mas'ter	
mas'tered	
mas'terful	
mas'tering	
mas'terly	
mas'terpiece	
mas'tery	
mas'ticate	

mas'ticated	
mastica'tion	
mas'turbate	
masturba'tion	
mat	
match	
match'ing	
match'less	
mate	
mate'rial	
mate'rialist	
materialis'tic	
mate'rialize	
mater'nal	
mater'nity	
mathemat'ic	
mathemat'- ical	
mathemat'- ically	
mathemati'cian	
mathemat'ics	
mat'inée	
matric'ulate	
matric'ulated	
matricula'tion	
matrimo'nial	
mat'rimony	
ma'trix	
ma'tron	
ma'tronly	
mat'ter	
mat'ting	
mat'tress	
mature'	
matured'	
matu'rity	
maul	
mauled	
mausole'um	
mauve	
max'im	
max'imize	
max'imum	
may (May)	
may'be	
mayonnaise'	
may'or	

may'oral	med'ley
may'oralty	meek
may'oress	meek'ly
maze	meet
me	meet'ing
mead'ow	megaloman'ia
mea'gre	meg'aphone
meal	meg'aton
meal'time	mel'ancholy
mean	mel'low
mean'est	mel'lowed
mean'ingless	melo'dious
meant	melodra'ma
mean'time	mel'ody
mean'while	mel'on
mea'sles	melt
meas'urable	melt'ed
meas'ure	melt'ing
meas'ured	mem'ber
meas'urement	mem'bership
meat	mem'brane
mechan'ic	memen'to
mechan'ical	mem'oir
mechan'- ically	mem'orable
mech'anism	memoran'da
mechaniza'tion	memoran'dum
mech'anize	memo'rial
med'al	mem'orize
med'dle	mem'orized
med'dled	mem'orizing
med'dlesome	mem'ory
me'dial	men
me'diate	men'ace
media'tion	men'aced
me'diator	men'acing
med'ical	menag'erie
medic'inal	mend
med'icine	menda'cious
medie'val	mend'ed
me'diocre	men'dicant
medioc'rity	mend'ing
med'itate	me'nial
med'itated	men'opause
medita'tion	men'tal
med'itative	mental'ity
Mediterra'nean	men'tion
me'dium	men'tioned

men'tioning
men'u

mer'cantile
mer'cenary
mer'chandise
mer'chant
mer'ciful
mer'cifully
mer'ciless
mer'cury
mer'cy
mere
mere'ly
merge
mer'ger
merid'ian
meri'no
mer'it
merito'rious
mer'riment
mer'ry
mesh
meshed
mes'merize
mes'merized
mess
mes'sage
mes'senger
met
metab'olism
met'al
metal'lic
metall'urgy
met'aphor
metaphor'ical
metapsych'ics
mete
me'teor
meteor'ic
me'ter
meth'ane
meth'od
method'ical
Meth'odist
metic'ulous
me'tre
met'ric

met'rical
metrop'olis
metropol'itan
met'tle
Mex'ican
mias'ma
mi'ca
mice
Mich'aelmas
mi'crobe
microb'iol'ogy
mic'rofilm
mi'crophone
mi'croscope
microscop'ic
mi'crowave
mid
mid'day
mid'dle
mid'dle-aged
mid'dle-class
mid'dleman
midg'et
mid'night
midst
mid'summer
mid'way
mid'winter
mien
might
might'y
mi'grant
mi'grate
mi'grated
mil'age
mild
mild'er
mild'est
mil'dew
mild'ly
mild'ness
mile
mile'age
mile'stone
mil'ieu
mil'itant
mil'itarism

militaris'tic	mirac'ulous
mil'itary	mirage'
mil'itate	mire
mil'itated	mir'ror
mili'tia	mirth
milk	mirth'ful
mill	mi'ry
millen'nium	misapplied'
mill'er	misapply'
mill'ibar	misapprehend'
mil'liner	misapprehen'-
mil'linery	sion
mil'lion	misappropria'-
millionaire'	tion
mill'stone	misbehave'
mim'ic	misbeha'viour
mince	
mind	miscal'culate
mind'ed	miscal'culated
mind'ful	miscalcula'tion
mine	miscar'ry
mi'ner	miscella'neous
min'eral	miscel'lany
min'gle	mischance'
min'iature	mis'chief
min'imal	mis'chievous
min'imize	misconcep'tion
min'imum	(miscon'duct, n.
mi'ning	(misconduct', v.
min'ion	misconstruc'-
min'ister	tion
min'istered	miscon'strue
ministe'rial	misdeed'
min'istering	misdemean'-
ministra'tion	our
min'istry	misdirect'
mi'nor	mi'ser
minor'ity	mis'erable
min'ster	mis'ery
min'strel	misfit'
mint	misfor'tune
mint'ed	misgiv'ing
mi'nus	misguide'
minus'cule	misguid'ed
min'ute, n., v.	mishap'
minute', adj.	misinform'
minu'tiae	misinformed'
mir'acle	misinter'pret

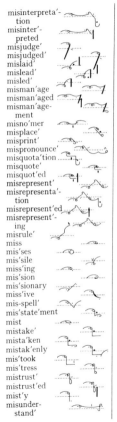

misinterpreta'-
tion
misinter'-
preted
misjudge'
misjudged'
mislaid'
mislead'
misled'
misman'age
misman'aged
misman'age-
ment
misno'mer
misplace'
misprint'
mispronounce'
misquota'tion
misquote'
misquot'ed
misrepresent'
misrepresenta'-
tion
misrepresent'ed
misrepresent'-
ing
misrule'
miss
mis'ses
mis'sile
miss'ing
mis'sion
mis'sionary
miss'ive
mis-spell'
mis'state'ment
mist
mistake'
mista'ken
mistak'enly
mis'took
mis'tress
mistrust'
mistrust'ed
mist'y
misunder-
stand'

misunder-
stand'ing
misunder'stood
misuse', v.
misuse', n.
mite
mit'igate
mit'igated
mitiga'tion
mix
mixed
mix'er
mix'ture
mnemon'ic
moan
mob
mobbed
mo'bile
mobil'ity
mobiliza'tion
mo'bilize
mock
mock'ery
mode
mod'el
mod'elled,
mod'eled
mod'erate,
n., a.
moderate', v.
mod'erately
modera'tion
mod'erator
mod'ern
mod'ernist
modernis'tic
moderniza'-
tion
mod'ernize
mod'est
mod'estly
mod'esty
mod'icum
modifica'tion
Moham'-
medan
Mo'hawk
Mohi'can

moi'ety
moist
mois'ten
mois'tened
mois'ture
mo'lar
molas'ses
mold
mol'ecule
mole'hill
molest'
molesta'tion
molest'ed
molest'ing
mol'lify
mol'ten
mo'ment
mo'mentarily
mo'mentary
momen'tous
momen'tum
mon'arch
monar'-
    chical
mon'archist
mon'astery
Mon'day
mon'etary
mon'etize
mon'ey
mon'key

mon'ogram
mon'ologue
mon'oplane
monop'olist
monop'olize
monop'oly
monot'onous
monot'ony
monox'ide
monsoon'
mon'ster
monstros'ity
mon'strous
mon'tage
month
month'ly

mon'ument
monumen'-
    tal
monumen'-
    tally
mood
mood'ily
mood'y
moon
moon'light
moon'shine
moor
moored
moor'land
mop
mope
mo'ped
mor'al
morale'
mor'alist
moral'ity
mor'alize
mor'alizing
mor'ally
morass'
morato'rium
mor'bid
morbid'ity
more
*more*o'ver
mor'ibund
morn
morn'ing
moroc'co
morose'
morose'ly
mor'phia
mor'row
mor'sel
mor'tal
mortal'ity
mor'tar
mort'gage
mort'gaged
mortgagee'
mort'gager
mort'gaging
mort'gagor

mortifica'tion	
mor'tified	
mor'tify	
mor'tuary	
mosa'ic	
mosqui'to	
moss	
moss'y	
most	
most'ly	
mote	
motel	
moth	
moth'er	
mo'ther-craft	
moth'erhood	
moth'er-*in*-law	
mo'tion	
mo'tioned	
mo'tionless	
mot'ivate	
motiva'tion	
mo'tive	
mot'ley	
mo'tor	
mo'tor-bus	
mo'tor-car	
mo'tor-cy'cle	
mo'torist	
mot'orway	
mot'tled	
mot'to	
mould	
mould'ed	
mould'er	
mould'ing	
mould'y	
mound	
mount	
moun'tain	
mountaineer'	
moun'tainous	
mount'ebank	
mourn	
mourn'er	
mourn'ful	

mourn'fully	
mourn'ing	
mouse	
mouse'-ear	
mouse'hole	
moustache'	
mouth	
mouth'ful	
mouth'piece	
mov'able, move'able	
move	
moved	
move'ment	
mov'er	
mow (to grimace)	
mow (to cut)	
mow (of hay)	
mowed	
mow'er	
Mr.	
Mrs.	
much	
mud	
mud'dle	
mud'dled	
mud'dy	
muf'fle	
muf'fled	
muf'ti	
mug	
mulat'to	
mul'berry	
mulct	
mulct'ed	
mule	
multifa'rious	
mul'tiple	
multiplica'tion	
multiplic'ity	
mult'iplied	
mul'tiply	
mul'titude	
multitu'dinous	
mum'ble	
mumps	
munch	

mun'dane	mu'tilate
munic'ipal	mu'tilated
municipal'ity	mutila'tion
munif'icence	mu'tiny
munif'icent	mut'ter
munif'icently	mut'tered
muni'tion	mut'tering
mu'ral	mut'ton
mur'der	mu'tual
mur'dered	muz'zle
mur'derer	muz'zled
mur'deress	my
mur'derous	myr'iad
mur'mur	myrrh
mur'mured	myr'tle
mur'muring	myself'
mus'cle	myste'rious
mus'cular	myste'riously
muse	mys'tery
mused	mys'tic
muse'um	mys'tical
mush'room	mys'tically
mu'sic	mys'ticism
mu'sical	mystifica'tion
musi'cian	mys'tified
mus'ketry	mys'tify
Muslim	mys'tifying
mus'lin	mystique'
mus'quash	myth
mus'sel	myth'ical
must	myth'ically
mus'tard	mytholog'ic
mus'ter	mytholog'ical
mus'tered	mytholog'ically
mute	mythol'ogy

N

nag
nail
nailed
nail'ing
naïve', naive'
na'ked
name
named
name'less
name'ly
nap
naph'tha
nap'kin
narcot'ic
narrate'
narra'ted
narra'tion
nar'rative
narra'tor
nar'row
nar'rowed
nar'rower
nar'rowest
nar'rowing
nar'rowly
nar'row-
minded
na'sal
nas'ty
na'tal
na'tion
na'tional
na'tionalist
national'ity
nationaliza'-
tion
na'tionalize
na'tionally
na'tive
nativ'ity

nat'ural
nat'uralist
naturaliza'tion
nat'uralize
nat'uralized
nat'urally
na'ture
na'turism
naught
naugh'ty
nau'sea
nau'seate
nau'tical
na'val
nave
nav'igable
nav'igate
nav'igated
naviga'tion
nav'igator
nav'vy
na'vy
nay
near
neared
near'er
near'est
near'ing
near'ly
neat
neat'er
neat'est
neat'ly
neb'ulous
nec'essarily
nec'essary
neces'sitate
neces'sitated
neces'sitating
neces'sitous

129

neces'sity		nes'tle	
neck		nes'tled	
neck'lace		net	
neck'tie		net'ted	
neck'wear		net'ting	
nec'tar		net'tle	
need		net'tled	
need'ed		net'work	
need'ful		neural'gia	
nee'dle		neurasthe'nia	
need'less		neurasthen'ic	
need'lessly		neuri'tis	
need'lessness		neurot'ic	
nee'dlework		neu'ter	
nefa'rious		neu'tral	
nega'tion		neutral'ity	
neg'ative		neu'tralize	
neglect'		neut'ron	
neglect'ed		nev'er	
neglect'ful		nev'ermore	
neglect'ing		*nevertheless'*	
néglige'		new	
neg'ligence		new'comer	
neg'ligent		new'er	
neg'ligently		new'est	
neg'ligible		newfan'gled	
negotiabil'ity		new-fash'ioned	
nego'tiable		new'ly	
nego'tiate		news	
nego'tiated		news'agent	
negotia'tion		news'paper	
ne'gress		news'print	
ne'gro		next	
ne'groid		nib	
neigh		nib'ble	
neigh'bour,		nib'bled	
neigh'bor		nib'bling	
neigh'bour-		nice	
hood		nice'ly	
nei'ther		ni'cest	
Nem'esis		ni'cety	
ne'on		niche	
neph'ew		nick	
Nep'tune		nick'el	
nerve		nick'name	
nerv'ous		nic'otine	
nerv'ously		niece	
nest		nig'gardly	

nigh	
night	
night'gown	
night'ingale	
night'ly	
night'mare	
night'shirt	
night'wear	
nil	
nim'ble	
nine	
nineteen'	
nineteenth'	
nine'tieth	
nine'ty	
ninth	
nip	
nip'ple	
ni'trate	
ni'tre	
ni'tric	
ni'trogen	
nitrog'enous	
nit'wit	
no	
nobil'ity	
no'ble	
no'body	
noctur'nal	
nod	
nod'ded	
nod'ding	
nog'gin	
noise	
noise'less	
noise'lessly	
nois'ily	
nois'y	
nom'ad	
nomad'ic	
no'menclature	
nom'inal	
nom'inate	
nomina'tion	
nominee'	
non-accep'-tance	

non-appear'-ance	
non-arri'val	
non-attend'-ance	
non'chalance	
non'chalant	
non-com'-batant	
non-commis'-sioned	
non-commit'-tal	
non-deliv'ery	
non'descript	
none	
nonen'tity	
non-interven'-tion	
non-par'ty	
nonpay'ment	
non'plussed	
non-res'ident	
non'sense	
nonsen'sical	
non'-stop	
nook	
noon	
noon'day	
nor	
nor'mal	
Nor'man	
north	
north-east'	
north-east'er	
north-east'ern	
north'erly	
north'ern	
north'erner	
north'ward	
north-west'	
north-west'er	
north-west'-erly	
north-west'ern	
Norwe'gian	

nose		no'wise	
nos'tril		nox'ious	
not		noz'zle	
notabil'ity		nucleon'ics	
no'table		nu'cleus	
no'tary		nude	
nota'tion		nudge	
notch		nu'dism	
note		nu'dist	
note'book		nug'get	
note'worthy		nui'sance	
noth'ing		null	
no'tice		nul'lified	
no'ticeable		nul'lify	
no'ticed		nul'lity	
no'ticing		numb	
not'ifiable		numbed	
notifica'tion		num'ber	
no'tified		num'bered	
no'tify		num'bering	
no'tion		nu'meral	
notori'ety		numer'ical	
noto'rious		nu'merous	
notwithstand'-		nun	
ing		nup'tials	
nought		nurse	
noun		nursed	
nour'ish		nurs'ery	
nour'ished		nur'ture	
nour'ishment		nur'tured	
nov'el		nut	
nov'elist		nu'triment	
nov'elty		nutri'tion	
Novem'ber		nutri'tional	
nov'ice		nutri'tious	
now		nut'shell	
now'adays		nyl'on	
no'where		nymph	

O

O (*oh*)		obscured'	
oak		obscu'rity	
oar		obse'quious	
oa'sis			
oath		observ'ance	
oat'meal		observ'ant	
oats		observa'tion	
ob'duracy		observe'	
ob'durate		observed'	
ob'durately		observ'er	
obe'dience		observ'ing	
obe'dient		obsess'	
obe'diently		obsessed'	
obese'		obses'sion	
obes'ity		obsoles'cence	
obey'		ob'solete	
obey'ing		ob'stacle	
obit'uary		ob'stinacy	
{ob'ject, *n.*		ob'stinate	
{object', *v.*		obstrep'erous	
object'ed		obstruct'	
object'ing		obstruct'ed	
objec'tion		obstruct'ing	
objec'tionable		obstruc'tion	
objec'tive		obstruc'tive	
objec'tively		obtain'	
obliga'tion		obtain'able	
		obtained'	
ob'ligatory		obtain'ing	
oblige'		obtrude'	
obliged'		obtru'ded	
oblique'		obtru'ding	
oblit'erate		obtru'sion	
oblit'erated		obtru'sive	
oblitera'tion		obtru'sively	
obliv'ion		obtuse'	
obliv'ious		ob'viate	
ob'long		ob'viated	
obnox'ious		ob'viating	
obscure'		ob'vious	

ob'viously
occa'sion
occa'sional
occa'sioned
occa'sioning
oc'cident
occiden'tal
oc'cupancy
oc'cupant
occupa'tion
oc'cupied
oc'cupier
oc'cupy
oc'cupying
occur'
occurred'
occur'rence
occur'ring
o'cean
o'clock'
oc'tagon
octag'onal
oc'tane
oc'tave
Octo'ber
oc'ulist
odd
o'dious
o'dium
o'dorous
o'dour, o'dor
oes'trogen
oes'trum
of
off
offence'
offend'
offend'ed
offend'er
offend'ing
offen'sive
of'fer
off'hand
of'fice
of'ficer
offi'cial
offi'cially
offi'ciate

offi'ciated
offi'cious
offi'ciously
(off'set, n.
(offset', v.
off'spring
oft'en
oft'entimes
oh
oil
oil'cloth
oiled
oil'skin
oil'y
oint'ment
old
old'er
old'est
old-fash'ioned
ol'ive
om'elet,
    om'elette
o'men
om'inous
om'inously
omis'sion
omit'
omit'ted
omit'ting
om'nibus
omnip'otence
omnip'otent
omnis'cience
omnis'cient
omniv'orous
on
once
on'cost
one
on'erous
oneself'
one'sided
one'-way
on'ion
on'looker
on'ly
on'set
on'slaught

o'nus		o'ral	
on'ward		or'ange	
on'yx		ora'tion	
ooze		or'ator	
o'pal		or'atory	
opaque'		orb	
o'pen		or'bit	
open-air'		or'chard	
o'pened		or'chestra	
o'pener		orches'tral	
o'pening		or'chestrate	
o'penly		or'chid	
op'era		ordain'	
op'erate		ordained'	
operat'ic		or'deal	
opera'tion		or'der	
opera'tional		or'dered	
op'erative		or'dering	
op'erator		or'derliness	
operet'ta		or'derly	
opin'ion		or'dinal	
o'pium		or'dinance	
oppo'nent		or'dinarily	
opportune'		or'dinary	
opportu'nity		ord'nance	
oppose'		ore	
op'posite		or'gan	
opposi'tion		organ'ic	
oppress'		organ'ically	
oppressed'		or'ganism	
oppres'sion		or'ganist	
oppress'ive		organiza'tion	
oppress'ively		or'ganize	
oppress'or		or'ganizer	
op'tic		or'ganizing	
op'tical		or'gy	
opti'cian		o'rient	
op'timism		orien'tal	
op'timist		or'igin	
optimis'tic		orig'inal	
op'timum		original'ity	
op'tion		orig'inate	
op'tional		orig'inated	
op'ulence		orig'inating	
op'ulent		origina'tion	
op'us		orig'inator	
or			
or'acle			

or'nament	
ornamen'tal	
ornamenta'-tion	
ornate'	
or'phan	
or'thodox	
os'cillate	
oscilla'tion	
os'cillograph	
os'citancy	
osten'sibly	
ostenta'tion	
ostenta'tious	
os'teopath	
os'tracize	
os'trich	
oth'er	
oth'erwise	
ought	
ounce	
our	
ours	
ourselves'	
oust	
oust'ed	
oust'ing	
out	
out'board	
out'break	
out'burst	
out'cast	
out'come	
out'cry	
out'dated'	
outdoors'	
out'er	
out'fit	
out'fitter	
out'going	
out'ing	
outland'ish	
out'law	
out'lay	
out'let	
out'line	
out'look	
out'lying	

outnum'ber	
outnum'bering	
out-*of*-date'	
out-*of*-doors'	
out'put	
out'rage	
outra'geous	
out'right	
out'set	
out'side	
outsi'der	
out'size	
out'skirts	
outstand'ing	
outstretch'	
outstrip'	
outvote'	
out'ward	
out'wardly	
out'wards	
outwit'	
o'val	
ova'tion	
ov'en	
o'ver	
o'veralls	
overbal'ance	
overbal'anced	
overbear'ing	
o'verboard	
overbur'dened	
overcame'	
o'vercast	
{o'vercharge, *n.* / overcharge', *v.*	
o'vercoat	
overcome'	
overcom'ing	
over-con'fident	
overcrowd'ed	
overdo'	
{o'verdose, *n.* / overdose', *v.*	
o'verdraft	
overdrawn'	
overdue'	

{o'verflow, *n.*	
{overflow', *v.*	
overgrown'	
overhang'	
overhaul'	
overhauled'	
overhead'	
o'verheads	
overhear'	
overheard'	
overjoyed'	
o'verland	
{o'verload, *n.*	
{overload', *v.*	
overlook'	
o'verpass	
overpow'er	
o'verride'	
overruled'	
o'verseas'	
oversee'	
o'verseer	
overshad'ow	
o'vershoes	
o'versight	
o'verstaffed'	
overstep'	
overstrain'	
overtake'	
{o'vertax, *n.*	
{overtax', *v.*	

overthrow'	
overthrown'	
o'vertime	
overtook'	
o'verture	
overturn'	
{o'verweight, *n.*	
{overweight', *v.*	
overwhelm'	
{o'verwork, *n.*	
{overwork', *v.*	
owe	
owed	
owes	
ow'ing	
owl	
own	
owned	
own'er	
own'ership	
own'ing	
ox	
ox'en	
ox'ide	
oxidiza'tion	
ox'idize	
ox'ygen	
oys'ter	
oys'ter-shell	
o'zone	

P

pa
pace
paced
pacif'ic
pac'ified
pa'cifism
pa'cifist
pac'ify
pack
pack'age
pack'er
pack'et
pact
pad
pad'ded
pad'ding
pad'dle
pad'lock
pad'locked
paediat'rics
pa'gan
page
pag'eant
pag'eantry
paid
pail
pain
pained
pain'ful
pain'fully
pain'less
pains
pains'taking
paint
paint'ed
paint'er
paint'ing
pair
pal
pal'ace

pal'atable
pal'ate
pala'tial
pale
pal'ette
palisade'
pall
pal'liate
pallia'tion
pal'liative
pal'lid
pal'lor
palm
palm'ist
pal'mistry
palm'-oil
pal'pable
pal'pitate
pal'pitated
palpita'tion
pal'try
pam'per
pam'pered
pam'pering
pam'phlet
pan
panace'a
panama'
pandemo'nium
pan'der
pan'dered
pane
pan'el
pang
pan'ic
pan'ic-stricken
panora'ma
panoram'ic

pant
pantech'nicon
pant'ed
pan'tomime
pan'try
papa'
pa'pal
pa'per
papy'rus
par
par'able
par'achute
parade'
par'adise
par'adox
paradox'ical
par'affin
par'agon
par'agraph
par'allel
par'alleled
par'alyse
par'alysed
par'alysing
paral'ysis
paralyt'ic
par'amount
paranoi'a
par'apet
parapherna'lia
par'aphrase
par'asite
pa'rasites
parasol'
par'cel
par'cel(l)ed
parch
parch'ment
par'don
par'donable
pare
pa'rent
pa'rentage
paren'tal
paren'thesis
parenthet'ic
parenthet'ical

par'ish
parish'ioner
Paris'ian
par'ity
park
par'king
par'lance
par'ley
par'liament
parliamen'tary
par'lour
par'lous
paro'chial
par'ody
parole'
par'oxysm
(parquet', n.,
{ a.
(par'quet, v.
par'rot
par'ry
pars'ec
parsimo'nious
par'simony
pars'ley
pars'nip
par'son
part
partake'
part'ed
par'tial
partial'ity
partic'ipant
partic'ipate
partic'ipated
partic'ipating
participa'tion
par'ticle
partic'ular
partic'ularize
partic'ularly
part'ing
par'tisan
parti'tion
parti'tioned
parti'tionist

part'ly
part'ner
part'nership
part'-time
par'ty
pass
pass'able
pas'sage
passed
pas'senger
pas'sion
pas'sionate
pas'sive
pas'sively
pass'port
pass'word
past
paste
paste'board
pa'sted
pas'tel
pastiche'
pastille'
pas'time
past'mas'ter
pas'tor
pas'toral
pa'stry
pas'ture
pat
patch
pat'ent
pat'ented
patentee'
pater'nal
path
pathet'ic
pathet'ically
pa'thos
pa'tience
pa'tient
pa'tiently
pa'triarch
pat'riot
patriot'ic
pat'riotism
patrol'
patrolled'

pa'tron
pat'ronage
pat'ronize
pat'ter
pat'tern
pau'city
pau'per
pause
paused
paus'ing
pave
pave'ment
pavil'ion
pav'ing
paw
pawn
pawn'broker
pawned
pawn'shop
pay
pay'able
payee'
pay'er
pay'ing
pay'master
pay'ment
pea
peace
peace'able
peace'ful
peace'fully
peach
peak
peal
pealed
pear
pearl
peas'ant
peas'antry
peb'ble
peck
pecula'tion
pecu'liar
peculiar'ity
pecu'liarly
pecu'niary
ped'agogic
ped'agogy

ped'al
ped'ant
pedan'tic
ped'dle
ped'estal
pedes'trian
ped'igree
ped'lar
peek
peel
peeled
peel'ing
peep
peeped
peep'ing
peer
peer'age
peer'ing
pee'vish
pee'vishly
peg
pel'let
pellu'cid
pelt
pelt'ed
pen
pe'nal
pe'nalize
pen'alty
pen'ance
pence
pen'cil
pen'cil(l)ed
pend'ant
pend'ent
pend'ing
pen'dulous
pen'dulum
pen'etrate
pen'etrated
penetra'tion
penicill'in
penin'sula
pe'nis
pen'itence
pen'itent
peniten'tiary
pen'manship

pen'niless
pen'ny
pen'sion
pen'sioned
pen'sioner
pen'sioning
pen'sive
pent
penu'rious
pen'ury
peo'ple
peo'pled
pep
pep'per
pep'sin
per
peram'bulate
peram'bulator
per an'num
perceive'
per cent'
percent'age
percep'tible
percep'tion
perch
per'colate
per'colator
percus'sion
perdi'tion
per'emptory
peren'nial
per'fect
per'fected
perfec'tion
per'fectly
per'fidy
per'forate
perfora'tion
perform'
perform'ance
performed'
perform'er
perform'ing
/per'fume, *n.*
\perfume', *v.*
perfunc'tory

perhaps'	per'sonal
per'il	personal'ity
per'ilous	personifica'-
pe'riod	tion
period'ical	personnel'
per'iscope	perspec'tive
per'ish	perspicac'ity
per'ishable	perspicu'ity
per'ished	perspira'tion
per'jure	perspire'
per'jurer	persuade'
per'jury	persua'ded
per'manency	persua'sion
per'manent	persua'sive
per'manently	pert
per'meate	pertain'
permis'sible	pertained'
permis'sion	pertain'ing
(per'mit, n.	pertinac'ity
(permit', v.	per'tinent
per'mutate	perturb'
perni'cious	peru'sal
perox'ide	peruse'
perpendic'ular	pervade'
	perva'ded
per'petrate	perverse'
per'petrated	(per'vert, n.
perpet'ual	(pervert', v.
perpet'uate	pes'simism
perpet'uated	pes'simist
perpetu'ity	pessimis'tic
perplex'	pest
perplex'ity	pes'ter
per'quisite	pes'tered
per'secute	pes'tilence
persecu'tion	pes'tilent
per'secutor	pet
persever'ance	pet'al
persevere'	peti'tion
persevered'	peti'tioned
perseve'ringly	peti'tioner
Per'sian	pet'rified
persist'	pet'rify
persist'ence	pet'rol
persist'ent	petro'leum
persist'ently	pet'ted
persist'ing	pet'ticoat
per'son	pet'ty

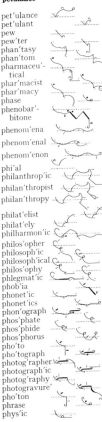

pet'ulance
pet'ulant
pew
pew'ter
phan'tasy
phan'tom
pharmaceu'-
  tical
phar'macist
phar'macy
phase
phenobar'-
  bitone
phenom'ena
phenom'enal
phenom'enon
phi'al
philanthrop'ic
philan'thropist
philan'thropy
philat'elist
philat'ely
philharmon'ic
philos'opher
philosoph'ic
philosoph'ical
philos'ophy
phlegmat'ic
phob'ia
phonet'ic
phonet'ics
phon'ograph
phos'phate
phos'phide
phos'phorus
pho'to
pho'tograph
photog'rapher
photograph'ic
photog'raphy
photogravure'
pho'ton
phrase
phys'ic

phys'ical
physi'cian
phys'icist
phys'ics
physiog'raphy
physiolog'ical
physiol'ogy
physiothe'rapist
physiothe'rapy
physique'
pi'anist
pian'o
pianofor'te
piaz'za
pick
pick'et
pick'le
pic'nic
picto'rial
pic'ture
picturesque'
pie
piece
piece'meal
piece'-work
pier
pierce
pierced
pi'ety
pig
pig'eon
pig'eonhole
pig'iron
pig'ment
pig'my
pile
pil'fer
pil'ferage
pil'fered
pil'ferer
pil'fering
pil'grim
pil'grimage
pill
pil'lage
pil'lar
pil'lion

pil'low	plac'id
pi'lot	pla'giarism
pin	pla'giarize
pin'cers	plague
pinch	plaid
pine	plain
pine'apple	plain'est
pin'ion	plain'ly
pin'ioned	plain'tiff
pink	plain'tive
pin'nacle	plait
pint	plait'ed
pin'-up	plan
pioneer'	plane
pi'ous	plan'et
pi'ously	plank
pip	planned
pipe	plant
pi'per	planta'tion
pi'quancy	plant'ed
pi'quant	plant'er
pique	plas'ter
pi'racy	plas'tered
pi'rate	plas'terer
pis'tol	plas'tic
pis'ton	plate
pit	plateau'
pitch	plat'form
pitch'er	plat'inum
pit'eous	plat'itude
pit'fall	platoon'
pith	plausibil'ity
pit'iable	plau'sible
pit'iful	play
pit'iless	played
pit'ilessness	play'er
pit'man	play'ful
pit'-saw	play'fulness
pit'tance	play'ground
pit'y	play'ing
piv'ot	play'mate
piv'otal	play'room
{plac'ard, *n.*	play'thing
{placard', *v.*	plea
placard'ed	plead
placate'	pleas'ant
place	pleas'antly
placed	please

pleas'urable	po'etry	
pleas'ure	poign'ancy	
pleat	poign'ant	
plea'ted	point	
plebe'ian	point'ed	
pledge	point'er	
ple'nary	point'ing	
plen'teous	point'less	
plen'tiful	poise	
plen'ty	poi'son	
pli'able	poi'sonous	
pli'ant	poke	
plied	po'lar	
pli'ers	pole	
plight	police'	
plod	police'-court	
plot	police'man	
plough	pol'icy	
ploughed	pol'io	
plough'ing	pol'ish	
pluck	pol'ished	
plug	polite'	
plum	pol'itic	
plu'mage	polit'ical	
plumb	politi'cian	
plumb'er	pol'itics	
plumb'ing	poll	
plumb'-rule	pollute'	
plume	pollu'tion	
plumed	pol'tergeist	
plump	polytech'nic	
plun'der	pol'ythene	
plun'dered	pomp	
plunge	pom'pous	
plu'ral	pond	
plus	pon'der	
plush	pon'dered	
ply	pon'derous	
pneumat'ic	pongee'	
pneumo'nia	pontoon'	
poach	po'ny	
pock'et	pool	
pock'et-book	pooled	
po'em	pool'ing	
po'et	poop	
po'etess	poor	
poet'ic	poor'er	
poet'ical	poor'est	

poor'house	possibil'ity
pop	pos'sible
pope	post
pop'lar	post'age
pop'lin	post'al
pop'pycock	post'card
pop'ulace	**post'code**
pop'ular	post'date
popular'ity	post'dated
popula'tion	post'er
pop'ulous	poster'ity
porce'lain	post'-free
porch	post-haste'
pore	post'humous
pork	post'ing
por'ous	post'man
por'poise	post'mark
por'ridge	post'master
port	**post'paid**
port'able	postpone'
port'al	postponed'
portend'	postpone'ment
por'tent	**postpon'ing**
porten'tous	post'script
port'er	pos'ture
portfo'lio	pot
port'hole	pot'ash
port'ico	potas'sium
port'ière	pota'to
por'tion	pota'toes
port'ly	po'tency
portman'teau	po'tent
por'trait	poten'tial
por'traiture	po'tion
portray'	pot'ter
portray'al	pot'tery
portrayed'	pouch
Portuguese'	poul'tice
pose	poul'try
poseur'	pounce
posi'tion	pounced
pos'itive	pounc'ing
pos'itively	pound
possess'	pour
possessed'	poured
posses'sion	pov'erty
possess'ive	pow'der
possess'or	pow'ders

pow'er
pow'erful
pow'erless

practicabil'ity
prac'ticable
prac'tical
{prac'tice
{prac'tise
prac'tised
prac'tising
practi'tioner
prai'rie
praise
praised
praise'worthy
prance
pranced
prank
pray
prayed
prayer
pray'ing
preach
preach'er
preach'ing
pream'ble
preca'rious
precau'tion
precau'tionary
precede'
prece'dence
prece'dent, a.
prec'edent, n.
pre'cept
pre'cinct
pre'cious
prec'ipice
precip'itate,
   n., a.
precip'itate, v.
precise'
precise'ly
precis'ion
preclude'
preco'cious
precoc'ity
preconceive'

predeces'sor
predic'ament
predict'
predict'able
predict'ed
predic'tion
predispose'
predom'inance
predom'inant
predom'inantly
predom'inate
pre-em'inence
pre-em'inent
pre'fab
pref'ace
pref'aced
prefer'
pref'erable
pref'erence
preferen'tial
preferred'
{pre'fix, n.
{prefix', v.
preg'nant
prehistor'ic
prej'udice
prej'udiced
prejudi'cial
prejudi'cially
prej'udicing
prel'ate
prelim'inary
prel'ude
premature'
premed'itate
premed'itated
premedita'tion
prem'ier
prem'ise, n.
premise', v.
pre'mium
pre-nat'al
prepaid'
prepara'tion
prepar'atory

prepare'	
prepared'	
prepar'ing	
prepon'der-ance	
prepon'derat-ing	
preposi'tion	
prepossess'ing	
prepos'terous	
prereq'uisite	
prerog'ative	
Presbyte'rian	
pres'bytery	
prescribe'	
prescribed'	
prescri'ber	
prescrip'tion	
pres'ence	
(pres'ent, n., a.	
(present', v.	
present'able	
presenta'tion	
pres'ently	
preserva'tion	
preserv'ative	
preserve'	
preserved'	
preside'	
pres'idency	
pres'ident	
presiden'tial	
presi'ding	
press	
pressed	
press'ing	
pres'sure	
prestige'	
presu'mably	
presume'	
presumed'	
presump'tion	
presump'tive	
presump'tuous	
pretence'	
pretend'	

pretend'ed	
pretend'ing	
preten'tious	
pre'text	
pret'ty	
prevail'	
prevailed'	
prevail'ing	
prev'alence	
prev'alent	
prevar'icate	
prevar'icator	
prevent'	
prevent'ed	
prevent'ing	
preven'tion	
pre'view	
pre'vious	
pre'viously	
prey	
price	
priced	
price'less	
prick	
prick'ly	
pride	
priest	
pri'marily	
pri'mary	
pri'mate	
prime	
pri'mer	
prime'val, primae'val	
prim'itive	
prim'rose	
prince	
prin'cess	
prin'cipal	
prin'cipally	
prin'cipalship	
prin'ciple	
print	
print'ed	
print'er	
print'ing	

pri'or	
prior'ity	
pris'on	
pris'oner	
pri'vacy	
pri'vate	
priva'tion	
priv'ilege	
prize	
probabil'ity	
prob'able	
prob'ably	
pro'bate	
proba'tion	
proba'tionary	
probe	
probed	
prob'lem	
problemat'ic	
proce'dure	
proceed'	
pro'cess	
pro'cessed	
proces'sion	
proclaim'	
proclaimed'	
proclama'tion	
procliv'ity	
procon'sul	
procras'tinate	
procrastina'- tion	
proc'tor	
procur'able	
procure'	
prod	
prod'igal	
prodig'ious	
prod'igy	
prod'uce, *n.*	
produce', *v.*	
produ'cer	
prod'uct	
produc'tion	
produc'tive	
produc'tively	
productiv'ity	
profane'	

profan'ity	
profess'	
professed'	
profes'sing	
profes'sion	
profes'sional	
profes'sional- ism	
profes'sor	
prof'fer	
prof'fered	
profi'ciency	
profi'cient	
profi'ciently	
pro'file	
prof'it	
prof'itable	
prof'ited	
profiteer'	
prof'ligate	
profound'	
profuse'	
profu'sion	
prog'eny	
proges'terone	
prognos'tic	
prognostica'- tion	
pro'gramme, pro'gram	
pro'gress, *n.*	
progress', *v.*	
progres'sive	
prohib'it	
prohib'ited	
prohib'iting	
prohibi'tion	
prohibi'tive	
pro'ject, *n.*	
project', *v.*	
project'ed	
project'ing	
projec'tion	
project'or	
proleta'rian	
proleta'riat	
prolif'erate	

prolif'ic	proportion'ate
pro'logue	propor'tionately
prolong'	propo'sal
prolonga'tion	propose'
prolonged'	proposed'
promenade'	proposi'tion
prom'inence	propound'
prom'inent	propound'ed
prom'inently	propri'etary
promiscu'ity	propri'etor
prom'ise	propri'ety
prom'issory	propul'sion
promote'	pro ra'ta
promo'ted	prosa'ic
promo'ter	prose
promo'tion	pros'ecute
prompt	pros'ecuted
prompt'ed	prosecu'tion
prompt'ing	pros'ecutor
prompt'itude	pros'pect, n.
prone	prospect', v.
pro'noun	prospec'ted
pronounce'	prospec'tive
pronounce'-	prospec'tus
ment	pros'per
pronuncia'tion	pros'pered
proof	prosper'ity
prop	pros'perous
propagan'da	⎧ pros'trate, a.
prop'agate	⎩ prostrate', v.
propaga'tion	prostra'ted
propel'	prostra'tion
propelled'	protect'
propel'ler	protec'tion
propen'sity	protec'tionist
prop'er	protect'or
prop'erly	pro'test, n.
prop'erty	protest', v.
proph'ecy, n.	Pro'testant
proph'esied	protesta'tion
proph'esy, v.	protest'ed
proph'et	protest'ing
prophet'ic	prot'on
propi'tiate	protract'
propi'tiated	protract'ed
propi'tious	protrude'
propor'tion	protrud'ed
	proud

proud'ly		publica'tion	
prove		public'ity	
proved		pub'licly	
prov'en		pub'lish	
prov'erb		pub'lished	
prover'bial		pub'lisher	
provide'		pub'lishing	
provi'ded		pud'ding	
prov'idence		pud'dle	
prov'ident		pu'erile	
prov'ince		puff	
provin'cial		pu'gilist	
provi'sion		pugna'cious	
provi'sional		pugnac'ity	
provi'so		puis'ne	
provoca'tion		pull	
provoc'ative		pulled	
provoke'		pulp	
provo'king		pul'pit	
prow'ess		pulsa'tion	
prowl		pulse	
prowled		pum'ice	
proxim'ity		pump	
prox'imo		pumped	
pru'dence		pump'ing	
pru'dent		punch	
pruden'tial		punch'-card	
pru'dently		punct'ual	
prune		punctual'ity	
Prus'sian		punct'uate	
pry		punct'uated	
psalm		punctua'tion	
pseu'do		punct'ure	
pseud'onym		pun'ish	
psychiat'ric		pun'ishment	
psychi'atrist		pu'nitive	
psychi'atry		pu'ny	
psycho'an'alyst		pup	
psycholog'ical		pu'pil	
psycholog'ically		pup'pet	
psychol'ogist		pur'chase	
psychol'ogy		pur'chaser	
psych'opath		pur'chase-tax	
psychother'apist		pure	
pto'maine		pure'ly	
pub'lic		purge	
pub'lican		purifica'tion	

pur'ified	
pur'ify	
pur'ity	
purloin'	
pur'ple	
{ pur'port, *n.*	
{ purport', *v.*	
pur'pose	
pur'poseful	
pur'posely	
purse	
purs'er	
pursu'ant	
pursue'	
pursued'	
pursu'er	

pursuit'	
purvey'	
push	
pushed	
put	
pu'trefied	
pu'trefy	
pu'trid	
put'ter	
put'ting	
put'ty	
puz'zle	
puz'zled	
puz'zling	
pyjam'as	
pyl'on	
pyr'amid	

Q

quack		qua'vering	
quacked		quay	
quad'rangle		quay'side	
quad'rant		queen	
quad'ruped		queen'ly	
quad'ruple		queer	
quadru'plicate		quell	
quaff		quelled	
		quench	
quag'mire		que'ried	
quail		quer'ulous	
quaint		que'ry	
quake		quest	
quaked		ques'tion	
qua'ker		ques'tionable	
		ques'tionably	
qualifica'tion		ques'tioned	
qual'ified		ques'tioning	
qual'ify		ques'tionnaire	
qual'ity		queue	
qualm		quib'ble	
quan'dary		quick	
quan'tify		quick'en	
quan'tity		quick'ened	
qua'rantine		quick'er	
quar'rel		quick'ly	
quar'reled,		quick'ness	
quar'relled		quick'sand	
quar'relsome		quick'silver	
quar'ry		quick'witted	
quart		quies'cent	
quar'ter		qui'et	
quar'terly		qui'eten	
quar'termaster		qui'etly	
quar'tern		qui'etness	
quartet'		qui'etude	
quar'to		quie'tus	
quartz		quill	
quash		quilt	
qua'ver		quinine'	
qua'vered			

153

quinquen'nial		quiv'ering	
quintess'ence		quiz	
quip		quizzed	
quire		quiz'zical	
quit		quoin	
quite		quon'dam	
quits		quo'rum	
quit'ted		quo'ta	
quit'ter		quota'tion	
quit'ting		quote	
quiv'er		quo'ted	
quiv'ered		quo'ting	

R

rab'bi	raid
rab'bit	rail
rab'ble	rail'head
rab'id	rail'ing
race	rail'lery
race'course	rail'road
raced	rail'way
race'horse	rai'ment
ra'cer	rain
ra'cial	rain'bow
ra'cialism	rain'drop
ra'cing	rain'fall
ra'cist	rain'ing
rack	rain'proof
rack'et	rain'-water
ra'dar	rain'y
ra'diance	raise
ra'diant	raised
ra'diate	rai'sin
ra'diated	rake
ra'diating	ral'lied
radia'tion	ral'ly
ra'diator	ral'lying
rad'ical	ram
ra'dii	ram'ble
ra'dio	ram'bler
radioac'tive	ramifica'tion
ra'diogram	rammed
radiol'ogist	ramp
rad'ishes	rampage'
rad'ium	ram'pant
ra'dius	ram'part
raf'fle	ram'shackle
raf'fled	ran
raft	ranch
raft'er	ran'cid
rag	ran'cour,
rage	ran'cor
rag'ged	rand
ra'ging	

155

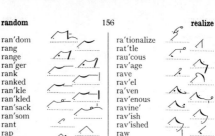

ran'dom	ra'tionalize
rang	rat'tle
range	rau'cous
ran'ger	rav'age
rank	rave
ranked	rav'el
ran'kle	ra'ven
ran'kled	rav'enous
ran'sack	ravine'
ran'som	rav'ish
rant	rav'ished
rap	raw
rapa'cious	ray
rapac'ity	raze
rap'id	ra'zor
rapid'ity	reach
rap'idly	reached
ra'pier	reach'ing
rapped	react'
rap'ping	react'ed
rapt	reac'tion
rap'ture	reac'tionary
rap'turous	reac'tor
rare	read
rare'ly	read, *p.t.*
rar'ity	read'able
ras'cal	readdress'
rascal'ity	read'er
rash	read'ier
rash'ly	read'ily
rasp	read'iness
rasp'berry	read'ing
rat	readjust'
rat'able	readjust'ed
ratch'et	readjust'ment
rate	readmis'sion
rate'able	readmit'
rate'payers	read'y
rath'er	read'ymade
ratifica'tion	reaffirm'
rat'ified	re'al
rat'ify	re'alism
ra'ting	re'alist
ra'tio	realist'ic
ra'tion	real'ity
ra'tional	re'alizable
rationaliza'-	realiza'tion
tion	re'alize

re'alized	recant'
re'alizing	recapit'ulate
re'ally	recapitula'tion
realm	recap'ture
ream	recast'
rean'imate	recede'
reap	rece'ded
reaped	rece'ding
reap'er	receipt'
reap'ing	receiv'able
reappear'	receive'
reappear'ance	received'
reappoint'	receiv'er
reappoint'ment	receiv'ership
reappor'tion	re'cent
rear	re'cently
reared	recep'tacle
re-arrange'	recep'tion
re-arrange'-ment	recep'tionist
rea'son	recep'tive
rea'sonable	receptiv'ity
rea'sonably	recess'
rea'soned	reces'sion
reassem'ble	reces'sional
reassert'	re'charge'
reassu'rance	rec'ipe
reassure'	recip'ient
re'bate, n.	recip'rocal
rebate', v.	recip'rocate
reb'el, n.	reciproca'tion
rebel', v.	reciproc'ity
rebelled'	reci'tal
rebell'ion	recita'tion
rebell'ious	recite'
rebound'	reci'ted
rebuff'	reci'ting
rebuild'	reck'less
rebuild'ing	reck'lessness
rebuilt'	reck'on
rebuke'	reck'oned
rebut'	reck'oning
rebut'tal	reclaim'
rebut'ting	reclaimed'
recal'citrant	reclama'tion
recall'	recline'
recalled'	reclined'
recall'ing	recli'ning
	recluse'

recogni'tion	rectan'gular
recog'nizance	rec'tify
recog'nizant	rec'tifying
rec'ognize	rec'titude
rec'ognized	rec'tor
recoil'	recum'bent
recoiled'	recu'perate
recollect'	recu'perated
recollec'tion	recu'perating
recommend'	recupera'tion
recommenda'- tion	recu'perative
rec'ompense	recur'
rec'oncile	recurred'
rec'onciled	recur'rence
reconcilia'tion	recur'rent
recondi'tion	recur'ring
reconnoi'tre	red
reconsid'er	redeem'
reconsidera'- tion	redeem'able
reconsid'ered	redeemed'
reconsid'ering	redemp'tion
reconstruct'	redeploy'
reconstruct'ed	red'-hot
reconstruct'ing	redistrib'ute
reconstruc'tion	red'olent
rec'ord, n.	redoub'le
record', v.	redound'
record'er	redound'ed
recount'	redraft'
recount'ed	redress'
recount'ing	reduce'
recoup'	reduced'
recourse'	redu'cing
recov'er	reduc'tion
recov'erable	redun'dant
recov'ered	re-ech'o
recov'ery	re-ech'oed
rec'reant	reed
rec'reate	reef
recrea'tion	reef'er
recrim'inate	reek
recrimina'tion	reel
recruit'	re-elect'
recruit'ed	re-elect'ed
recruit'ment	re'-elec'tion
rect'angle	reeled
	re-embark'
	re-enact'

re-enact'ment	refrig'erate
re-enforce'	refrig'erated
re-engage'	refrig'erating
re-en'ter	refrig'erate'tion
re-en'tered	refrig'erator
re-estab'lish	ref'uge
re-estab'- lished	refugee'
	refund'
re-estab'lish- ment	refund'ed
	refund'ing
re'-examina'- tion	refu'sal
	⎧ref'use, n., a.
re-exam'ine	⎩ refuse', v.
refer'	refuta'tion
referee'	refute'
ref'erence	refu'ted
referen'dum	refu'ting
	regain'
referred'	regained'
refer'ring	re'gal
refill'	regale'
refine'	regaled'
refine'ment	rega'lia
refi'ner	re'gally
refi'nery	regard'
refit'	regard'ed
reflect'	regard'ing
reflect'ed	regard'less
reflec'tion	re'gency
reflec'tive	regen'erate, n., adj.
reflect'or	
re'flex, n., adj.	regen'erate, v.
reflex', v.	regen'erated
reform'	regenera'tion
reforma'tion	re'gent
	régime'
reform'atory	reg'imen
reformed'	reg'iment
reform'er	regimen'tal
reform'ing	re'gion
refrac'tion	re'gional
	reg'ister
refrac'tory	reg'istered
refrain'	reg'istering
refrained'	reg'istrar
refresh'	registra'tion
refresh'ing	registrat'or
refresh'ment	reg'istry

regret'	
regret'ful	
regret'table	
regret'ted	
regret'ting	
reg'ular	
regular'ity	
reg'ularly	
reg'ulate	
reg'ulated	
reg'ulating	
regula'tion	
reg'ulator	
rehabil'itate	
rehabilita'tion	
rehears'al	
rehearse'	
rehearsed'	
rehears'ing	
reign	
reigned	
reimburse'	
reimbursed'	
reimburse'-ment	
rein	
reincarna'tion	
rein'deer	
reined	
reinforce'	
reinforced'	
reinforce'ment	
reinforc'ing	
reinsert'	
reinsert'ed	
reinspec'tion	
reinstate'	
reinstat'ed	
reinstate'ment	
reinstat'ing	
reinsur'ance	
reinsure'	
reinvest'	
reinvest'ment	
reis'sue	
reis'sued	

reit'erate	
reit'erated	
reitera'tion	
reject'	
reject'ed	
rejec'tion	
rejoice'	
rejoiced'	
rejoin'	
rejoin'der	
rejoined'	
relapse'	
relapsed'	
relate'	
rela'ted	
rela'tion	
rela'tionship	
rel'ative	
rel'atively	
relativ'ity	
relax'	
relax'ation	
relaxed'	
relay', n.	
re-lay', v.	
release'	
released'	
releas'ing	
rel'egate	
relega'tion	
relent'	
relent'ed	
relent'ing	
relent'less	
rel'evancy	
rel'evant	
reliabil'ity	
reli'able	
reli'ance	
reli'ant	
rel'ic	
relied'	
relief'	
relieve'	
relieved'	
reliev'ing	
relig'ion	

relig'ious	
relig'iously	
relin'quish	
relin'quished	
relin'quishing	
rel'ish	
rel'ished	
reluc'tance	
reluc'tant	
reluc'tantly	
rely'	
rely'ing	
remain'	
remain'der	
remained'	
remain'ing	
remand'	
remand'ed	
remark'	
remark'able	
remark'ably	
remarked'	
remark'ing	
reme'dial	
rem'edy	
remem'ber	
remem'bered	
remem'bering	
remem'brance	
remind'	
remind'ed	
remind'er	
remind'ing	
reminis'cence	
reminis'cent	
remiss'	
remis'sion	
remit'	
remit'tance	
rem'nant	
remod'el	
remon'strance	
remon'strant	
remon'strate	
remon'strated	
remon'strating	

remorse'	
remorse'ful	
remorse'less	
remote'	
remote'ly	
remov'able	
remov'al	
remove'	
removed'	
remov'ing	
remu'nerate	
remu'nerated	
remunera'tion	
remu'nerative	
rend	
ren'der	
ren'dered	
ren'dering	
ren'dezvous	
ren'egade	
renew'	
renew'al	
renewed'	
renew'ing	
renounce'	
renounced'	
ren'ovate	
renova'tion	
renown'	
renowned'	
rent	
rent'al	
rent'ed	
renum'bered	
renuncia'tion	
reoc'cupy	
reo'pen	
reorganiza'tion	
reor'ganize	
reor'ganized	
reor'ganizing	
reorienta'tion	
repaid'	
repair'	
repaired'	
repair'er	
repair'ing	
repara'tion	

repartee′	
repass′	
repast′	
repay′	
repay′able	
repay′ment	
repeal′	
repealed′	
repeat′	
repeat′edly	
repeat′ing	
repel′	
repelled′	
repel′lent	
repent′	
repent′ance	
repent′ant	
repent′ed	
repent′ing	
repercus′sion	
repertoire′	
rep′ertory	
repeti′tion	
repeti′tious	
repet′itive	
repine′	
repined′	
repi′ning	
replace′	
replace′able	
replace′ment	
replen′ish	
replen′ished	
replen′ishing	
replete′	
reple′tion	
rep′lica	
replied′	
reply′	
reply′ing	
report′	
report′ed	
report′er	
report′ing	
repose′	
repos′itory	
reprehend′	
reprehensible	

reprehen′sion	
represent′	
representa′tion	
represent′ative	
represent′ed	
represent′ing	
repress′	
repressed′	
repres′sion	
reprieve′	
reprieved′	
repriev′ing	
⎰rep′rimand, *n.*	
⎱reprimand′, *v.*	
⎰re′print, *n.*	
⎱reprint′, *v.*	
reprint′ed	
repri′sal	
reproach′	
reproached′	
reproach′ful	
reproach′fully	
reproach′ing	
rep′robate	
reproduce′	
reproduc′tion	
reproduc′tive	
reproof′	
reprove′	
reproved′	
rep′tile	
repub′lic	
repub′lican	
republica′tion	
repub′lish	
repub′lished	
repu′diate	
repu′diated	
repu′diating	
repudia′tion	
repug′nance	
repug′nant	
repulse′	
repulsed′	
repuls′ing	
repul′sion	

repul'sive		res'idency	
repul'sively		res'ident	
rep'utable		residen'tial	
reputa'tion		resid'ual	
repute'		resid'uary	
repu'ted		res'idue	
request'		resign'	
request'ed		resigna'tion	
request'ing		resigned'	
req'uiem		resign'ing	
require'		resil'ience	
required'		resil'iency	
require'ment		resil'ient	
requir'ing		res'in	
req'uisite		resist'	
requisi'tion		resist'ance	
requisi'tioned		resist'ed	
requisi'tioning		res'olute	
requi'tal		res'olutely	
requite'		resolu'tion	
requi'ted		resolve'	
re-read'		resolved'	
re-read', *p.t.*		resolv'ing	
rescind'		res'onance	
rescind'ed		res'onant	
res'cue		resort'	
res'cued		resort'ed	
res'cuer		resound'	
res'cuing		resound'ed	
research'		resource'	
resem'blance		resource'ful	
resem'ble		respect'	
resem'bled		**respect'ability**	
resent'		respect'able	
resent'ed			
resent'ful		respect'ably	
resent'ing		respect'ed	
resent'ment		respect'ful	
reserva'tion		respect'fully	
reserve'		**respect'ing**	
reserved'		**respect'ive**	
reserv'ing		**respect'ively**	
res'ervoir		respira'tion	
reset'			
reship'ment		res'pirator	
reside'		respir'atory	
resi'ded		res'pite	
res'idence		resplen'dent	

respond'	
respond'ed	
respon'der	
respond'ing	
response'	
responsibil'-ities	
(responsibil'-ity	
(respon'sible	
respon'sive	
rest	
res'taurant	
restau'rateur	
rest'ed	
rest'ful	
rest'fully	
rest'fulness	
rest'ing	
restitu'tion	
rest'ive	
rest'less	
rest'lessly	
rest'lessness	
restora'tion	
restor'ative	
restore'	
restored'	
restrain'	
restrained'	
restrain'ing	
restraint'	
restrict'	
restrict'ed	
restrict'ing	
restric'tion	
result'	
result'ant	
result'ed	
resume'	
résumé'	
resumed'	
resu'ming	
resump'tion	
resump'tive	
resurge'	
resurrec'tion	
resus'citate	

resuscita'tion	
re'tail, n., a.	
retail', v.	
retail'er	
retain'	
retained'	
retal'iate	
retal'iated	
retal'iating	
retalia'tion	
retard'	
retard'ed	
reten'tion	
reten'tive	
ret'icence	
ret'icent	
ret'ina	
ret'inue	
retire'	
retired'	
retire'ment	
retir'ing	
retort'	
retort'ed	
retouch'	
retrace'	
retraced'	
retra'cing	
retract'	
retreat'	
retreat'ed	
retreat'ing	
retrench'	
retrench'ment	
retribu'tion	
retrieve'	
retrieved'	
retriev'er	
retriev'ing	
ret'rograde	
ret'rograded	
ret'rospect	
retrospec'tion	
retrospec'tive	
retrospec'tively	
return'	
return'able	
returned'	

return'ing		revolt'	
reu'nion		revolt'ed	
reunite'		revolt'ing	
revalua'tion		revolu'tion	
reveal'		revolu'tionary	
revealed'		revolu'tionize	
reveal'ing		revolve'	
rev'el		revolved'	
revela'tion		revolv'er	
rev'elry		revul'sion	
revenge'		reward'	
revenged'		reward'ed	
revenge'ful		reward'ing	
rev'enue		rewrite'	
		rewrit'ten	
rever'berate		rhap'sody	
rever'berated		rhe'ostat	
reverbera'tion		rhes'us	
reverb'erator		rhet'oric	
revere'		rhetor'ical	
revered'		rheumat'ic	
rev'erence		rheum'atism	
rev'erend		rheu'matoid	
rev'erent			
rev'erie		rhinoc'eros	
revers'al		rhu'barb	
reverse'		rhyme	
reversed'		rhythm	
revers'ible		rhyth'mic	
revert'		rhyth'mical	
revert'ed		rib	
revert'ing		rib'ald	
review'		rib'bon	
reviewed'		rice	
review'er		rich	
review'ing		rich'er	
revile'		rich'es	
revise'		rich'est	
revised'		rich'ly	
revi'sing		rid	
revi'sion		rid'dance	
revi'sionary		rid'dle	
revi'sionist		ride	
revis'it		ri'der	
revi'val		ridge	
revive'		rid'icule	
revived'		rid'iculed	
revoke'		ridic'ulous	

ridic'ulously	ri'pened	
rid'ing	ri'pening	
rife	ripped	
riff'raff	rip'ping	
ri'fle	rip'ple	
ri'fled	rise	
ri'fling	ris'en	
rift	risibil'ity	
rig	ris'ible	
right	ri'sing	
right'-angle	risk	
right'-angled	risked	
right'eous	risk'ing	
right'eousness	risk'y	
right'ful	ris'qué	
right'fulness	rite	
right'-hand	rit'ual	
right'ing	ri'val	
right'ly	ri'val(l)ed	
rig'id	ri'val(l)ing	
rigid'ity	ri'valry	
rig'or	riv'er	
rig'orous	riv'et	
rig'our	riv'eted	
rile	riv'eting	
riled	road	
ri'ling	road'hog	
rim	road'side	
rime	road'ster	
rind	road'way	
ring	road'worthy	
ringed	roam	
ring'er	roamed	
ring'ing	roam'er	
ring'leader	roan	
ring'let	roar	
ring'-road	roared	
rink	roast	
rinse	roast'ed	
rinsed	roast'er	
rins'ing	roast'ing	
ri'ot	rob	
ri'oter	rob'ber	
ri'otous	rob'bery	
ri'otously	robe	
rip	rob'in	
ripe	rob'ot	
ri'pen	robust'	

robust'ly	rotate'
rock	rota'ted
rock'er	rota'tion
rock'ery	rote
rock'et	rot'ted
rock'ing	rot'ten
rod	rot'ting
rode	rotund'
ro'dent	rotund'ity
rode'o	rou'ble
roe	rouge
rogue	rough
rogu'ish	rough'en
rogu'ishly	rough'er
rôle	rough'ly
roll	round
rolled	round'about
roll'er	round'ed
roll'ing	round'ing
roll'ing-stock	round'ly
ro'man,	rouse
Ro'man	roused
romance'	rous'ing
roman'tic	rout
romp	route
romped	routine'
romp'ing	rove
rood	ro'ving
roof	ro'ver
roof'ing	row (a rank)
roof'less	row (a tumult)
room	row'diness
room'y	row'dy
roost	row'dyism
roost'er	rowed
root	row'lock
root'ed	roy'al
rope	roy'alist
ro'sary	roy'ally
rose	roy'alty
ro'seate	rub
ros'in	rubbed
ros'ter	rub'ber
ros'trum	rub'bing
ro'sy	rub'bish
rot	ru'by
Rotar'ian	ruc'tion
ro'tary	rudder

rude		run	
rude'ness		run'away	
ru'diment		run'-down'	
rudimen'tal		run'way	
rudimen'tary		rung	
rue		run'ner	
rued		run'ning	
rue'ful		rupee'	
rue'fully		rup'ture	
ruf'fian		rup'tured	
ruf'fle		ru'ral	
ruf'fled		ruse	
ruf'fling		rush	
rug		rushed	
rug'ged		rush'ing	
ru'in		rusk	
ruina'tion		rus'set	
ru'ined		Rus'sian	
ru'ining		rust	
ru'inous		rus'tic	
rule		rus'ticate	
ruled		rust'ing	
ru'ler		rus'tle	
ru'ling		rus'tled	
rum		rus'tling	
rumble		rust'y	
ru'minate		rut	
rum'mage		ruth	
ru'mour,		ruth'less	
ru'mor		ruth'lessly	
rump		ruth'lessness	
rum'ple		rye	
rum'pled		ry'ot	

S

Sab'bath		sal'ad	
sa'ble		sal'aried	
sabotage'		sal'ary	
sa'bre		sale	
sack		sale'able	
sack'ing		sales'man	
sac'rament		sales'manship	
sa'cred		sales'woman	
sac'rifice		sa'lient	
sac'rificed		salin'ity	
sac'rilege		sal'low	
sacrile'gious		sall'y	
sad		salm'on	
sad'den		saloon'	
sad'der		salt	
sad'dest		salt'ed	
sad'dle		salt'ing	
sad'dled		salu'brious	
sad'dler		sal'utary	
sa'dism		saluta'tion	
sad'ly		salute'	
safa'ri		salu'ted	
safe		sal'vage	
safe-con'duct		salva'tion	
safe'-depos'it		salve	
safe'guard		salved	
saf'er		Samar'itan	
saf'est		same	
safe'ty		sam'ple	
saga'cious		sanato'rium	
sagac'ity		sanc'tified	
sage		sanc'tify	
said		sanc'tion	
sail		sanc'tioned	
sailed		sanc'tioning	
sail'ing		sanc'tity	
sail'or		sanc'tuary	
saint		sanc'tum	
saint'ly		sand	
sake		san'dal	

169

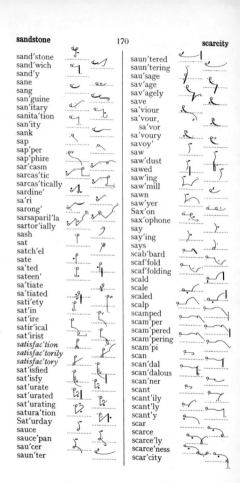

sand'stone	saun'tered
sand'wich	saun'tering
sand'y	sau'sage
sane	sav'age
sang	sav'agely
san'guine	save
san'itary	sa'viour
sanita'tion	sa'vour,
san'ity	sa'vor
sank	sa'voury
sap	savoy'
sap'per	saw
sap'phire	saw'dust
sar'casm	sawed
sarcas'tic	saw'ing
sarcas'tically	saw'mill
sardine'	sawn
sa'ri	saw'yer
sarong'	Sax'on
sarsaparil'la	sax'ophone
sartor'ially	say
sash	say'ing
sat	says
satch'el	scab'bard
sate	scaf'fold
sa'ted	scaf'folding
sateen'	scald
sa'tiate	scale
sa'tiated	scaled
sati'ety	scalp
sat'in	scamped
sat'ire	scam'per
satir'ical	scam'pered
sat'irist	scam'pering
satisfac'tion	scam'pi
satisfac'torily	scan
satisfac'tory	scan'dal
sat'isfied	scan'dalous
sat'isfy	scan'ner
sat'urate	scant
sat'urated	scant'ily
sat'urating	scant'y
satura'tion	scar
Sat'urday	scarce
sauce	scarce'ly
sauce'pan	scarce'ness
sau'cer	scar'city
saun'ter	

scare		scientif'ic	
scare'monger		scientif'ically	
scarf		sci'entist	
sca'ring		scin'tillating	
scar'let		scis'sors	
scarred		scoff	
scathe		scoffed	
sca'thing		scoff'er	
scat'ter		scoff'ing	
scat'tered		scold	
scat'tering		scone	
scenar'io		scoop	
scene		scoot'er	
sce'nery		scope	
sce'nic		scorch	
scent		score	
scent'ed		scored	
scep'tic,		scor'er	
skep'tic		scor'ing	
scep'tical		scorn	
scep'ticism		scorn'ful	
scep'tre		scorn'fully	
sched'ule		scorn'ing	
sched'ule (U.S.)		Scot	
sched'uled		Scotch, scotch	
scheme		Scots'man	
sche'mer		Scot'tish	
schizophren'ia		scoun'drel	
schnör'kel		scour	
		scourge	
schol'ar		scout	
schol'arly		scowl	
schol'arship		scowled	
scholas'tic		scowl'ing	
school		scram'ble	
school'boy		scram'bled	
schooled		scram'bling	
school'fellow		scrap	
		scrape	
school'girl		scratch	
school'house		scrawl	
school'master		scrawled	
school'mistress		scream	
school'room		screamed	
school'teacher		screech	
schoon'er		screen	
sciat'ica		screened	
sci'ence		screw	

screwed	
scrib'ble	
scrib'bled	
scrim'mage	
scrip	
script	
Scrip'ture	
scriv'ener	
scroll	
scrounge	
scrub	
scrubbed	
scru'ple	
scru'pulous	
scru'pulously	
scru'pulous- ness	
scru'tinize	
scru'tiny	
scuf'fle	
scuf'fled	
scull	
scull'er	
scull'ery	
sculp'tor	
sculp'ture	
scum	
scur'ried	
scur'rilous	
scur'ry	
scut'tle	
scythe	
sea	
sea'board	
sea'borne	
sea'-coast	
sea'faring	
seal	
sealed	
sea'-level	
seal'skin	
seam	
sea'man	
sea'manship	
seamed	
sea'plane	
sea'port	
search	

search'er	
search'ing	
search'light	
sea'shore	
sea'side	
sea'son	
sea'sonable	
sea'sonal	
sea'soned	
seat	
seat'ed	
seat'ing	
sea'ward	
sea'weed	
sea'worthy	
secede'	
seclude'	
seclu'sion	
seclu'sive	
Sec'onal	
sec'ond	
sec'ondary	
sec'onded	
sec'onder	
sec'ond-hand	
sec'ondly	
sec'ond-rate	
sec'onds	
se'crecy	
se'cret	
secreta'rial	
secreta'riat	
sec'retary	
secrete'	
secre'ted	
secre'tion	
se'cretive	
sect	
secta'rian	
sec'tion	
sec'tional	
sec'tionalize	
sec'tor	
sec'ular	
secure'	
secured'	
secure'ly	
secu'ring	

secu'rity	self'ish
sedate'	self'ishly
sed'entary	self'ishness
sed'iment	self-possessed'
sedi'tion	self-posses'sion
sedi'tious	
see	self-reli'ance
seed	self-respect'
see'ing	self-service'
seek	self-willed'
seem	sell
seemed	sell'er
seem'ingly	Sel'lotape
seen	selves'
seethe	sem'aphore
seeth'ing	sem'blance
seg'ment	sem'ibreve
seg'regate	sem'icircle
segrega'tion	sem'icolon
segrega'tionist	sem'inar
seismol'ogy	sem'inary
seize	sen'ate
seized	sen'ator
seiz'ing	send
sei'zure	send'er
sel'dom	se'nile
select'	senil'ity
select'ed	se'nior
select'ing	senior'ity
selec'tion	sensa'tion
select'ive	sensa'tional
select'or	sense
self	sense'less
self-addressed'	sense'lessly
self'-assur'ance	sense'lessness
self-con'fidence	sensibil'ity
	sen'sible
self-con'scious	sen'sitive
self-contained'	sen'sitively
self-control'	sen'sitiveness
self-defence'	sen'sual
self-determina'-	sent
tion	sen'tence
self-esteem'	sen'tenced
self-ev'ident	sen'tient
self-explan'-	sen'timent
atory	sentimen'tal
self-in'terest	sen'tinel

sen'try
sep'arate, *adj.*
sep'arate, *v.*
sep'arated
sep'arating
separa'tion
sep'arator
Septem'ber
sep'tic
sepul'chral
sep'ulchre
se'quel
se'quence
seques'tered
serenade'
serene'
serene'ly
seren'ity
serge
ser'geant
se'rial
seria'tim
se'ries
se'rious
se'riously
se'riousness
ser'jeant
ser'mon
serv'ant
serve
served
serv'ice
serv'iceable
serv'ile
servil'ity
serv'ing
serv'itude
ses'sion
set
set'back
set'ting
set'tle
set'tled
set'tlement
set'tler
set'tling
sev'en
seventeen

seventeenth'
sev'enth
sev'entieth
sev'enty
sev'er
sev'eral
sev'erally
sev'erance
severe'
sev'ered
severe'ly
sev'ering
sever'ity
sew
sew'age
sewed
sew'er
sew'erage
sew'ing
sewn
sex
sex'ton
sex'y
shab'by
shack
shack'le
shack'led
shade
shad'ow
shad'owy
sha'dy
shaft
shaft'ing
shake
sha'ken
sha'ker
sha'ky
shall
shal'low
shal'lower
sham
shame
shamed
shame'ful
shame'fully
shame'less
shampoo'
shampooed'

shampoo'ing	
sham'rock	
shape	
shape'less	
share	
shared	
share'holder	
sha'ring	
shark	
sharp	
sharp'en	
shar'pened	
shar'pening	
sharp'er	
sharp'est	
sharp'ly	
shat'ter	
shat'tered	
shave	
shaved	
shav'ing	
shawl	
she	
sheaf	
shear	
sheared	
shear'ing	
shears	
sheath	
sheathe	
sheaves	
shed	
sheen	
sheep	
sheep'ish	
sheep'ishly	
sheer	
sheet	
sheet'ing	
shelf	
shell	
shellac'	
shellacked'	
shelled	
shell'fish	
shel'ter	
shel'tered	
shel'tering	

shelve	
shemoz'zle	
shep'herd	
sher'bet	
sher'iff	
sher'ry	
shield	
shield'ed	
shield'ing	
shift	
shift'ed	
shift'ing	
shift'less	
shift'y	
shil'ling	
shim'mer	
shim'mered	
shim'mering	
shin	
shine	
shin'gle	
shi'ning	
shi'ny	
ship	
ship'builder	
ship'building	
ship'ment	
ship'owner	
ship'per	
ship'ping	
ship'yard	
shire	
shirk	
shirked	
shirk'er	
shirk'ing	
shirt	
shiv'er	
shiv'ered	
shiv'ering	
shoal	
shock	
shod	
shod'dy	
shoe	
shoe'maker	
shone	

shook		shrine	
shoot		shrink	
shoot'ing		shrink'age	
shop		shrink'ing	
shop'keeper		shriv'el	
shop'ping		shroud	
shop'-stew'ard		shroud'ed	
shore		shrub	
shorn		shrug	
short		shrunk	
short'age		shrunk'en	
short'bread		shud'der	
short'-circ'uit		shud'dered	
short'coming		shuf'fle	
short'en		shuf'fled	
short'er		shun	
short'est		shunt	
short'hand		shunt'ed	
short'ly		shunt'ing	
shorts		shut	
short'sighted		shut'ter	
short'-term		shut'tle	
shot		shy	
should		shy'ly	
shoul'der		sick	
shout		sick'en	
shout'ed		sick'le	
shout'ing		side	
shove		side'board	
shov'el		side'-car	
shov'el(l)ed		side'-effect	
show		side'light	
show'down		si'ding	
showed		si'dle	
show'er		siege	
show'ered		sieve	
show'ering		sift	
show'ing		sift'ed	
show'manship		sigh	
shown		sighed	
show'room		sigh'ing	
show'y		sight	
shrank		sight'seeing	
shrap'nel		sight'seer	
shred		sign	
shrewd		sig'nal	
shriek		sig'natory	
shrill		sig'nature	

sign'board		sin'ewy	
signed		sin'ful	
sign'er		sin'fully	
signif'icance		sing	
signif'icant		singe	
signif'icantly		singed	
significa'tion		singe'ing	
sig'nified		sing'er	
sig'nify		sing'ing	
sig'nifying		sin'gle	
sign'ing		sin'gle-handed	
sign'post		sin'gular	
sign'writer		singular'ity	
si'lence		sin'ister	
si'lencer		sink	
si'lent		sin'ner	
si'lently		sip	
silhouette'		si'phon	
silicos'is		sip'ping	
silk		sir	
sil'ly		sire	
sil'ver		si'ren	
sil'verware		sir'loin	
sim'ilar		sis'al	
similar'ity		sis'ter	
sim'ilarly		sis'ter-*in*-law	
sim'ile		sit	
simil'itude		site	
sim'mer		sit'ter	
sim'mered		sit'ting	
sim'mering		sit'uate	
sim'per		sit'uated	
sim'pered		situa'tion	
sim'ple		six	
sim'pler		six'fold	
simplic'ity		six'pence	
simplifica'tion		sixteen'	
sim'plify		sixteenth'	
sim'ulate		sixth	
sim'ulated		six'ty	
simulta'neous		size	
sin		size'able	
since		skate	
sincere'		ska'ted	
sincere'ly		ska'ter	
sincer'ity		ska'ting	
si'necure		skel'eton	
sin'ew		sketch	

sketched	slapped
sketch'ily	slap'ping
sketch'ing	slash
sketch'y	slashed
skew	slash'ing
skew'er	slate
ski	slaugh'ter
skid	slaugh'tered
skid'ding	slaugh'ter-
skiff	house
skil'ful	slave
skill	sla'very
skilled	sla'vish
skim	sla'vishly
skimmed	slay
skimp	slay'er
skin	sledge
skinned	sleek
skin'ning	sleep
skip	sleep'er
skipped	sleep'ily
skip'per	sleep'ing
skir'mish	sleep'less
skir'mished	sleep'lessness
skirt	sleep'y
skull	sleet
sky	sleeve
sky'lark	sleigh
sky'light	sleight
sky'scraper	slen'der
sky'way	slept
slab	sleuth
slack	slew
slack'en	slice
slack'ened	sliced
slag	slick
slain	slid
sla'lom	slide
slam	slide'-rule
slan'der	sli'ding
slan'dered	slight
slan'dering	slight'est
slan'derous	slight'ly
slang	slim
slant	slime
slant'ed	sling
slant'ing	slink
slap	slip

slip'per	
slip'pery	
slip'ping	
slip'road	
slip'shod	
slit	
slo'gan	
slope	
slot	
sloth	
sloth'ful	
slot'ted	
slouch	
slough (a bog)	
slough (a cast skin)	
slov'enly	
slow	
slow'ly	
slow'ness	
slug	
slug'gard	
slug'gish	
slug'gishly	
sluice	
slum	
slum'ber	
slum'bered	
slum'bering	
slump	
slung	
slur	
slurred	
slur'ring	
slush	
sly	
smack	
small	
small'er	
small'est	
smart	
smart'en	
smart'er	
smart'est	
smart'ly	
smash	
smashed	
smat'ter	

smat'tering	
smear	
smeared	
smear'ing	
smell	
smelled	
smelt	
smelt'ed	
smelt'er	
smile	
smiled	
smi'lingly	
smith	
smog	
smoke	
smo'ker	
smooth	
smooth'er	
smote	
smoth'er	
smoth'ered	
smoul'der	
smoul'dered	
smudge	
smug'gle	
smug'gled	
smug'gler	
snack'-bar	
snag	
snail	
snake	
snap	
snapped	
snap'shot	
snare	
snared	
sna'ring	
snarl	
snarled	
snatch	
snatched	
snatch'ing	
sneak	
sneer	
sneered	
sneer'ing	
sneeze	
sniff	

sniv'el	soiled
snob	soj'ourn
snob'bery	sol'ace
snob'bish	so'lar
snoop	sold
snoop'er	sol'der
snore	sol'dered
snort	sol'dier
snow	sole
snow'drift	sole'ly
snowed	sol'emn
snow'fall	solem'nity
snow'shoes	solemniza'tion
snow'storm	sol'emnize
snub	sol'emnly
snuff	solic'it
snug	solicita'tion
so	solic'ited
soak	solic'itor
soaked	solic'itous
soap	solic'itude
soar	sol'id
soared	solidar'ity
sob	solid'ified
so'ber	solid'ify
sobri'ety	solid'ity
so'-called	sol'idly
socc'er	
sociabil'ity	solil'oquize
so'ciable	
so'cial	solil'oquized
so'cialism	solil'oquy
so'cialist	sol'itary
socialist'ic	sol'itude
soci'ety	so'lo
sociol'ogy	so'loist
sociom'etry	solubil'ity
sock	sol'uble
sock'et	solu'tion
sod	solve
so'da	solved
so'fa	solv'ency
soft	solv'ent
sof'ten	som'bre
sof'tener	some
soft'ly	some'body
soft'wood	some'how
soil	some'one
	som'ersault

some'thing	
some'time	
some'what	
some'where	
son	
song	
song'ster	
son'ic	
son'-*in*-law	
son'net	
sonor'ity	
sono'rous	
sono'rously	
soon	
soon'er	
soot	
soothe	
soothed	
sooth'ing	
sop	
sophis'ticated	
sophistica'tion	
soporif'ic	
sopra'no	
sor'did	
sor'didness	
sore	
sor'row	
sor'rowful	
sor'rowfully	
sor'rowing	
sor'ry	
sort	
sort'ed	
sort'er	
sort'ing	
sought	
soul	
sound	
sound'ed	
sound'er	
sound'est	
sound'ing	
sound'proof	
sound'track	
soup	
sour	
source	

soured	
south	
south-east'	
south-east'ern	
south'erly	
south'ern	
south'erner	
south'ward	
south-west'	
south-west'ern	
souvenir'	
sov'ereign	
sov'ereignty	
Sov'iet	
sow (pig)	
sow (to scatter)	
sowed	
sow'er	
sow'ing	
sown	
space	
spaced	
space'-man	
space'-ship	
space'-station	
space'-suit	
spa'cious	
spa'ciously	
spade	
span	
span'gle	
Span'iard	
span'iel	
Span'ish	
spanned	
spar	
spare	
spared	
spar'ing	
spar'ingly	
spark	
spark'le	
spark'led	
spark'ling	
spar'row	
sparse	
sparse'ly	
spar'sity	

Spar'tan	spell'bound
spasm	spelled
spasmod'ic	spell'ing
spasmod'ically	spelt
spat	spend
spate	spend'ing
spat'ter	spend'thrift
speak	spent
speak'er	sphere
speak'ing	spher'ical
spear	sphinx
spe'cial	spice
spe'cialist	spi'der
special'ity	spike
specializa'tion	spill
spe'cialize	spilled
spe'cially	spilt
spe'cialty	spin
spe'cie	spin'ach
spe'cies	spi'nal
specif'ic	spin'dle
specif'ically	spine
specifica'tion	spin'ster
spec'ified	spi'ral
spec'ify	spire
spec'ifying	spir'it
spec'imen	spir'ited
spe'cious	spir'itual
speck	spit
spec'tacle	spite
spectac'ular	spite'ful
specta'tor	spite'fulness
spec'tre	splash
spectrom'eter	splashed
spec'ulate	splash'ing
spec'ulated	spleen
spec'ulating	splen'did
specula'tion	splen'didly
spec'ulative	splen'dour
spec'ulator	splice
sped	splint
speech	splin'ter
speed	splin'tered
speed'ily	splin'tering
speedom'eter	split
speed'way	splutter'
speed'y	splut'tered
spell	splut'tering

spoil	spur	
spoiled	spu'rious	
spoilt	spurn	
spoke	spurned	
spo'ken	spurn'ing	
spokes'man	spurred	
sponge	spurt	
spon'sor	spy	
spon'sored	spy'ing	
spontane'ity	squab'ble	
sponta'neous	squad	
spool	squad'ron	
spoon	squal'id	
sporad'ic	squall	
sport	squall'y	
sport'ing	squal'or	
sports'man	squan'der	
sports'manship	squan'dered	
sports'wear	squan'dering	
spot	square	
spot'-check	squash	
spot'less	squaw	
spouse	squeak	
spout	squeal	
sprain	squeam'ish	
sprained	squeeze	
sprain'ing	squint	
sprang	squire	
sprawl	squirm	
sprawled	squir'rel	
sprawl'ing	squirt	
spray	stab	
spread	stabbed	
spread'ing	stabil'ity	
sprig	sta'bilize	
spright'ly	sta'bilizer	
spring	sta'ble	
spring'ing	stack	
spring'time	sta'dium	
sprin'kle	staff	
sprin'kled	stag	
sprint	stage	
sprout	stage'craft	
sprout'ed	stag'ger	
spruce	stag'gered	
sprung	stag'gering	
spry	stag'nant	
spun	stagna'tion	

staid	stain	stained	stain'less	stair	stair'case	stair'way	stake	staked	stale	stalk	stalked	stalk'er	stall	stal'wart	stam'ina	stam'mer	stam'mered	stam'mering	stamp	stamped	stampede'	stanch	stand	stand'ard	standardiza'-tion	stand'ardize	stand'-by'	stand'-in	stand'ing	stand'point	stand'still	sta'ple	star	starch	starch'iness	stare	stared	sta'ring	stark	star'ring	star'ry	start	start'ed	start'er	start'le	start'led

start'ling	starva'tion	starve	starved	starv'ing	state	sta'ted	state'less	state'ly	state'ment	state'room	states'man	states'manlike	states'manship	stat'ic	stat'ically	sta'ting	sta'tion	sta'tionary	sta'tioned	sta'tioner	sta'tionery	statis'tical	statis'tically	statisti'cian	statis'tics	stat'ue	stat'ure	sta'tus	stat'ute	stat'utory	staunch	stave	stay	stayed	stay'ing	stead	stead'fast, sted'fast	stead'fastly	stead'ied	stead'ier	stead'iest	stead'ily	stead'y	steak	steal	stealth

stealth'y	
steam	
steam'boat	
steamed	
steam'er	
steam'roller	
steam'ship	
steed	
steel	
steel'yard	
steep	
stee'ple	
steer	
steer'age	
steered	
steer'ing	
stem	
stench	
sten'cil	
sten'cilled	
sten'cilling	
stenog'rapher	
stenograph'ic	
stenog'raphy	
sten'tor	
stento'rian	
step	
step'-ladder	
stepped	
step'ping	
step'ping-stone	
ster'eotyped	
ster'ile	
steril'ity	
steriliza'tion	
ster'ilize	
ste'rilizer	
ster'ling	
stern	
stern'er	
stern'est	
stern'ly	
stet	
steth'oscope	
ste'vedore	
stew	
stew'ard	

stew'ardess	
stew'ardship	
stich, stick	
stiff	
stiff'en	
stiff'ened	
sti'fle	
sti'fled	
sti'fling	
stig'ma	
stig'matize	
still	
stim'ulant	
stim'ulate	
stim'ulated	
stim'ulating	
stimula'tion	
stim'ulus	
sting	
stint	
stint'ed	
stint'ing	
sti'pend	
stip'ulate	
stip'ulated	
stip'ulating	
stip'ulation	
stir	
stirred	
stir'ring	
stir'rup	
stitch	
stitched	
stitch'ing	
stock	
stock'broker	
stock'holder	
stock'ing	
stock'ist	
stock'list	
stock'pile	
stock'piling	
stock'taking	
stodg'y	
Stoic	
sto'ical	
sto'icism	
stoke	

stok'er		strait'en	
stok'ing		strait'ened	
stole		strand	
sto'len		strand'ed	
stol'id		strange	
stom'ach		strange'ly	
stone		stran'ger	
stood		stran'gle	
stooge		stran'glehold	
stool		strap	
stoop		straphang'er	
stop		stra'ta	
stop'page		strat'agem	
stop'ping		strateg'ic	
stor'age		strat'egy	
store		strat'osphere	
stored		stra'tum	
store'keeper		straw	
stor'ing		straw'berry	
storm		straw'board	
stor'y		stray	
stout		strayed	
stout'er		streak	
stout'est		stream	
stout'heart'ed		streamed	
stout'ly		stream'ing	
stove		stream'line	
stow		street	
stow'age		strength	
stow'away		strength'en	
stowed		strength'ened	
stow'ing		strength'ening	
strad'dle		stren'uous	
strag'gler		stren'uously	
straight		Streptococ'cus	
straight'away		streptomy'cin	
straight'en		stress	
straight'ened		stretch	
straight'ening		stretch'er	
straight'er		stretch'ing	
straight'est		strew	
straightfor'- ward		strewed	
		strick'en	
strain		strict	
strained		strict'er	
strain'er		strict'est	
strain'ing		strict'ly	
strait		stric'ture	

stride		
stri'dent		
strife		
strike		
stri'ker		
stri'king		
string		
strin'gency		
strin'gent		
strip		
stripe		
strip'tease		
strive		
strode		
stroke		
stroll		
strolled		
strong		
stron'ger		
stron'gest		
strong'hold		
strong'ly		
strong'minded		
strong'room		
strop		
strove		
struck		
struc'tural		
struc'ture		
strug'gle		
strug'gled		
strug'gling		
strung		
strut		
strut'ted		
strych'nia		
strych'nine		
stub'born		
stub'bornness		
stuc'co		
stuck		
stud		
stud'ded		
stu'dent		
stud'ied		
stu'dio		
stu'dious		
stud'y		

stud'ying		
stuff		
stum'ble		
stum'bled		
stum'bling		
stum'bling- block		
stump		
stumped		
stun		
stunned		
stung		
stunt		
stunt'ed		
stupefac'tion		
stu'pefy		
stupen'dous		
stu'pid		
stupid'ity		
stu'pidly		
stu'por		
stur'dy		
stut'ter		
stut'tered		
stut'tering		
style		
styled		
styl'i		
sty'lish		
sty'lishly		
sty'lo		
suave		
subal'tern		
subaquat'ic		
subcommit'- tee		
subdivide'		
subdivi'sion		
subdue'		
subdued'		
subed'it		
sub'hu'man		
{sub'ject, a. {subject', v.		
subject'ed, p.p.		
subject'ing		
subjec'tion		
subjec'tive		

subjec'tively
subjoin'
subjoined'
sublet'
sublime'
sublim'ity
sub'marine
submerge'
submers'ible
submis'sion
submiss'ive
submit'
submit'ted
submit'ting
subnor'mal
subor'dinate,
  n., a.
subor'dinate, *v.*
subordina'tion
suborn'
subpoe'na
subscribe'
subscribed'
subscri'ber
subscri'bing
subscrip'tion
sub'sequent
sub'sequently
subserv'ient
subside'
subsi'ded
subsi'dence
subsid'iary
sub'sidize
sub'sidized
sub'sidizing
sub'sidy
subsist'
subsist'ed
subsist'ence
subson'ic
sub'stance
substan'tial
substan'-
  tially
substan'tiate
substan'tiated

substantia'-
  tion
sub'stitute
sub'stituted
substitu'tion
subsume'
sub'terfuge
subterra'nean
sub'tle
sub'tlety
subtract'
subtract'ed
subtrac'tion
sub'urb
subur'ban
suburb'ia
sub'urbs
sub'way
succeed'
succeed'ed
succeed'ing
success'
success'ful
success'fully
succes'sion
succes'sive
succes'sively
success'or
succinct'
suc'cour,
  suc'cor
succumb'
succumbed'
such
suck
suck'le
suc'tion
sud'den
sud'denly
sud'denness
sue
sued
suède
su'et
suf'fer
suf'ferance
suf'fered
suf'ferer

suffice'
sufficed'
suffi'ciency
suffi'cient
suffi'ciently
{ suf'fix, *n.*
{ suffix', *v.*
suf'focate
suf'focated
suf'focating
suffoca'tion
suf'frage
sug'ar
suggest'
suggest'ed
suggest'ing
sugges'tion
suggest'ive
suici'dal
su'icide
su'ing
suit
suitabil'ity
suit'able
suite
suit'ed
suit'ing
sulk'y
sul'len
sul'lenness
sul'phate
sul'phide
sul'phur
sulphu'ric
sul'tan
sul'try
sum
sum'marily
sum'marize
sum'mary
summed
sum'mer
sum'mit
sum'mon
sum'moned
sum'mons
sump'tuous
sump'tuously

sun
sun'bathe
sun'beam
sun'burn
sun'burnt
Sun'day
sun'der
sun'dry
sung
sunk
sunk'en
sun'light
sun'lit
sun'rise
sun'set
sun'shine
sun'spot
sup
su'per
su'perable
superabun'-
    dance
superabun'-
    dant
superan'nuate
superan'nua-
    ted
superannua'-
    tion
superb'
supercil'ious
superfi'cial
su'perfine
superflu'ity
super'fluous
superhu'man
superintend'
superintend'ed
superintend'-
    ence
superintend'-
    ent
supe'rior
superior'ity
super'lative
super'latively
su'permarine
su'permarket

supernat'ural	surf
supersede'	sur'face
superse'ded	surf'-board
superse'ding	sur'feit
superson'ic	sur'feited
supersti'tion	surge
supersti'tious	surged
supervise'	sur'geon
supervised'	sur'gery
supervi'sion	sur'gical
supervi'sor	sur'ly
sup'per	surmise'
supplant'	surmised'
supplant'ed	surmount'
supplant'ing	surmount'able
sup'ple	surmount'ed
sup'plement	surmount'ing
supplemen'tal	sur'name
supplemen'-tary	surpass'
sup'pliant	surpassed'
sup'plicant	sur'plus
sup'plicate	surprise'
supplica'tion	surprised'
supplied'	surpri'sing
supply'	surre'alism
support'	surren'der
support'able	surren'dered
support'ed	surrepti'tious
support'er	surround'
support'ing	surround'ed
suppose'	surround'ing
supposed'	{sur'tax, n.
suppo'sing	{surtax', v.
supposi'tion	{sur'vey, n.
suppress'	{survey', v.
suppressed'	surveyed
suppress'ing	survey'ing
suppres'sion	survey'or
suprem'acy	survi'val
supreme'	survive'
supreme'ly	survived'
{sur'charge, n.	survi'ving
{surcharge', v.	survi'vor
sure	susceptibil'ity
sure'ly	suscep'tible
sur'est	
sur'ety	suscep'tibly
	sus'pect, n.

suspect', *v.*	swelled
suspect'ed	swell'ing
suspend'	swel'ter
suspend'ed	swel'tered
suspend'ing	swept
suspense'	swerve
suspen'sion	swerved
suspi'cion	swerv'ing
suspi'cious	swift
suspi'ciously	swift'er
sustain'	swift'est
sustained'	swift'ly
sustain'ing	swim
sus'tenance	swim'mer
su'ture	swim'ming
su'tured	swim'mingly
swag'ger	swin'dle
swal'low	swin'dled
swal'lowed	swin'dler
swal'lowing	swin'dling
swam	swine
swamp	swing
swamped	swing'ing
swamp'y	Swiss
swan	switch
swap	switch'board
swarm	switched
swarmed	switch'ing
swarm'ing	swiv'el
swarth'y	swoll'en
swathe	swoon
sway	swoop
swayed	sword
sway'ing	swore
swear	sworn
sweat	swung
sweat'er	syc'amore
Swede	syllab'ic
Swe'dish	syl'lable
sweep	syl'labus
sweep'er	syl'van
sweep'ing	sym'bol
sweet	symbol'ic
sweet'er	sym'bolize
sweet'est	symmet'rical
sweet'ly	symmet'rically
sweet'ness	sym'metry
swell	sympathet'ic

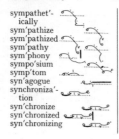

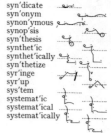

sympathet'-
   ically
sym'pathize
sym'pathized
sym'pathy
sym'phony
sympo'sium
symp'tom
syn'agogue
synchroniza'-
   tion
syn'chronize
syn'chronized
syn'chronizing

syn'dicate
syn'onym
synon'ymous
synop'sis
syn'thesis
synthet'ic
synthet'ically
syn'thetize
syr'inge
syr'up
sys'tem
systemat'ic
systemat'ical
systemat'ically

T

tab
tab'ernacle
ta'ble
tableau'
ta'ble-cloth
ta'blespoon

ta'blespoon'ful

tab'let
ta'bleware
tab'loid
taboo'
tab'ular
tab'ulate
tab'ulated
tab'ulating
tabula'tion
tab'ulator
tac'it
tac'iturn
tack
tacked
tack'le
tack'led
tact
tact'ful
tact'fully
tac'tical
tactic'ian
tac'tics
tact'less
taff'eta
tag
tail
tail'or
tail'ored
tail'oring
taint
taint'ed
taint'ing

take
ta'ken
take'-over
ta'king
talc
tale
tal'ent
tal'ented
tal'isman
talk
talk'ative
talk'er
talk'ing
tall
tall'er
tallest
tal'lied
tal'low
tal'ly
tame
tamed
ta'mer
tam'per
tam'pered
tam'pering
tan
tan'dem
tan'gent
tan'gible
tan'gle
tang'o
tank
tank'ard
tan'ker
tan'ner
tan'nery
tan'nic
tan'nin
tan'talize
tan'talizing

tan'tamount	taunt'ing	
tan'trum	taut	
tap	tav'ern	
tape	taw'dry	
ta'per	taw'ny	
tape'-record'er	tax	
ta'pering	tax'able	
tap'estry	taxa'tion	
tapio'ca	taxed	
tapped	tax'-free	
tap'ping	tax'i	
tar	tax'icab	
tar'dily	tax'payer	
tar'diness	tea	
tar'dy	teach	
tare	teach'er	
tar'get	teach'ing	
tar'iff	tea'cup	
tar'mac	teak	
tar'nish	team	
tar'nished	tea'pot	
tarpau'lin	tear, *n.*	
tar'ried	tear, *v.*	
tar'ring	tear'ful	
tar'ry, *adj.*	tear'ing	
tar'ry, *v.*	tease	
tart	tea'spoon	
tar'tan	tea'spoonful	
tar'tar	tech'nical	
tartar'ic	technical'ity	
task	tech'nically	
tas'sel	technique'	
taste	technol'ogist	
ta'sted	technol'ogy	
taste'ful	te'dious	
taste'fully	te'diously	
taste'less	te'dium	
taste'lessness	tee	
ta'sting	teem	
ta'sty	teemed	
tat'ter	teem'ing	
tat'tered	teen'age	
tat'tle	teen'ager	
tattoo'	teeth	
tattooed'	teethe	
taught	teeto'tal	
taunt	teeto'taler,	
taunt'ed	teeto'taller	

tel'ecast	tempt'ing
telegen'ic	ten
tel'egram	ten'able
tel'egraph	tena'cious
telegraph'ic	tena'ciously
teleg'raphist	tenac'ity
teleg'raphy	ten'ancy
telep'athy	ten'ant
tel'ephone	tend
telephon'ic	tend'ed
teleph'onist	ten'dency
teleph'ony	ten'der
tele'photo	ten'dered
tel'eprinter	ten'dering
telepromp'ter	ten'derly
tel'escope	tend'ing
telescop'ic	ten'don
tele'type	ten'ement
tel'eview	ten'et
tele'vise	ten'fold
tel'evision	ten'nis
tell	ten'or
tell'er	tense
tell'ing	tense'ly
tell'-tale	ten'sion
temer'ity	tent
tem'per	ten'tacle
tem'perament	ten'tative
tempera-men'tal	ten'tatively
tempera-men'tally	tenth
tem'perance	ten'ure
tem'perate	tep'id
tem'perately	term
tem'perature	termed
tem'pered	ter'minable
tem'pering	ter'minal
tem'pest	ter'minate, *a.*
tempes'tuous	ter'minate, *v.*
tem'ple	ter'minated
tem'poral	termina'tion
	ter'minus
tem'porarily	ter'race
tem'porary	ter'ra-cot'ta
tempt	terrain'
tempta'tion	ter'rible
tempt'ed	ter'ribly
	ter'rier
	terrif'ic

ter'rified
ter'rify
territo'rial
ter'ritory
ter'ror
ter'rorism
ter'rorize
terse
terse'ly
terylene'
test
tes'tament
testamen'tary
testa'tor
testa'trix
test'ed
test'er
tes'tified
tes'tify
testimo'nial
tes'timony
test'ing
tes'ty
teth'er
teth'ered
text
text'book
tex'tile
tex'ture
than
thank
thanked
thank'ful
thank'fully
thank'fulness
thank'ing
thank'less
thanks
thanks'giving
that
thatch
thatched
thaw
thawed
the
the'atre,
the'ater
theat'rical

theft
their
theirs
them
theme
themselves'
then
thence
thenceforth'
thencefor'ward
theolog'ical
theolog'-
ically
theol'ogist
theol'ogy
the'orem
theoret'ical
theoret'ically
the'orist
the'orize
the'ory
there
there'about
*there*af'ter
*there*at'
*there*by'
there'for
there'fore
*there*from'
*there*in'
*there*of'
*there*on'
*there*out'
*there*to'
*there*upon'
*there*with'
therm
thermion'ic
thermom'eter
ther'mos
ther'mostat
these
the'sis
they
thick
thick'en
thick'ened
thick'ening

thick'er	
thick'et	
thick'ly	
thick'ness	
thief	
thieves	
thigh	
thim'ble	
thin	
thine	
thing	
think	
think'er	
think'ing	
thin'ly	
thinned	
thin'ner	
third	
third'ly	
third'-rate'	
thirds	
thirst	
thirst'ed	
thirst'ing	
thirst'y	
thirteen'	
thirteenth'	
thir'tieth	
thir'ty	
this	
this'tle	
thorn	
thorn'y	
thor'ough	
thor'oughbred	
thor'oughfare	
thor'oughly	
thor'oughness	
those	
thou	
though	
thought	
thought'ful	
thought'fully	
thought'ful- ness	
thought'less	
thought'lessly	

thought'less- ness	
thou'sand	
thou'sandfold	
thrash	
thrashed	
thrash'ing	
thread	
thread'bare	
thread'ed	
thread'ing	
threat	
threat'en	
threat'ened	
three	
three- quarters	
thresh	
thresh'old	
threw	
thrice	
thrift	
thrift'y	
thrill	
thrilled	
thrill'er	
thrill'ing	
thrive	
thri'ving	
throat	
throb	
throbbed	
throb'bing	
throne	
throng	
thronged	
throng'ing	
throt'tle	
through	
throughout'	
throw	
throw'back	
throw'ing	
thrown	
thrust	
thrust'ing	
thud	
thumb	

thump	tint
thumped	tint'ed
thun'der	tint'ing
thun'dered	ti'ny
Thurs'day	tip
thus	tip'off
thwart	tipped
thwart'ed	tip'ping
tick'et	tirade'
tick'le	tire
ti'dal	tired
tide	tire'less
ti'ded	tire'some
ti'dings	tir'o
ti'dy	tis'sue
tie	Titan'ic
tied	tit'-bit
tier	tithe
ti'ger	ti'tle
tight	tit'ter
tight'en	tit'ular
tight'ened	to
tight'ening	toast
tight'ly	toast'ed
tight'ness	toast'ing
tile	tobac'co
tiled	tobac'conist
till, n. and v.	tobog'gan
till, prep.	today'
tilt	toe
tilt'ed	tof'fee,
tilt'ing	tof'fy
tim'ber	togeth'er
time	toil
time'keeper	toiled
time'table	toi'let
tim'id	tok'en
timid'ity	told
tim'idly	tol'erable
tim'orous	tol'erably
tin	tol'erance
tinc'ture	tol'erant
tinge	tol'erate
tin'gle	tol'erated
tin'kle	tol'erating
tinned	tolera'tion
tin'plate	toll
tin'sel	tolled

toma'to
tomb
tomb'stone
tomor'row
ton
tone
tongs
tongue
ton'ic
tonight'
ton'nage
too
took
tool
tooth
tooth'ache
top
to'paz
top'-heavy
top'ic
top'ical
top'ple
top'pled
top'pling
torch
tore
{tor'ment, n.
{torment', v.
torment'ed
torment'ing
torn
torna'do
torpe'do
tor'pid
tor'rent
torren'tial
tor'rid
tor'toise
tor'tuous
tor'ture
tor'tured
tor'turing
toss
tossed
toss'ing
to'tal
to'tally
tote

tot'ter
touch
touched
touch'ing
tough
tough'en
tough'er
tough'est
tough'ness
tour
tour'ing
tour'ism
tour'ist
tour'nament
tour'ney
tout
tout'ed
tout'ing
tow
to'ward
to'wards
towed
tow'el
tow'er
tow'ered
tow'ering
tow'ing
town
town'-clerk'
town'ship
towns'man
tox'ic
toy
toyed
trace
trace'able
traced
tra'cer
tra'cing
track
tracked
track'less
tract
tract'able
trac'tion
trac'tor
trade
tra'ded

trade'-mark	*trans'*fer, *n.*
tra'der	*transfer'*, *v.*
*trades'*man	trans'ferable
trades-u'nion	trans'ference
	transferred'
trades-u'nion-	
ism	transfix'
trade-u'nion	transform'
tra'ding	
tradi'tion	transforma'-
tradi'tional	tion
tradi'tionally	
traf'fic	transform'er
trag'edy	
trag'ic	transgress'
trag'ically	transgressed'
trail	transgress'ing
trail'er	transgres'sion
trail'ing	tranship'
train	tranship'ment
trainee'	tran'sient
train'er	transist'or
train'ing	trans'it
trait	transi'tion
trai'tor	transi'tional
tram	trans'itory
tramp	translate'
tramped	transla'ted
tramp'ing	transla'ting
tram'ple	transla'tion
tram'pled	transla'tor
tram'pling	transmis'sion
trance	transmit'
tran'quil	transmit'ted
tranquil'lity	transmit'ter
transact'	transmit'ting
transact'ed	transpa'rent
transact'ing	transpire'
transac'tion	transpired'
transatlan'tic	transpi'ring
transcend	transplant'
transcend'ed	trans'port, *n.*
transcend'ence	transport', *v.*
transcend'ent	transporta'-
transcribe'	tion
transcribed'	transport'ed
tran'script	transpose'
transcrip'tion	transship'
	transship'ment
	trap

trap'-door'	tri'bal
trapeze'	tribe
trapped	tribula'tion
trap'ping	tribu'nal
trash	trib'une
trav'el	trib'utary
trav'elled, trav'eled	trib'ute
trav'eller, trav'eler	tri'ceps
trav'elogue	trick
trav'erse	tricked
trav'ersed	trick'ery
treach'erous	trick'le
treach'ery	trick'led
treac'le	trick'y
tread	tried
tread'ing	trien'nial
trea'son	tri'fle
treas'ure	tri'fled
treas'urer	tri'fling
treas'ury	trig'ger
treat	trim
treat'ed	trim'ly
treat'ing	trimmed
trea'tise	trin'ity
treat'ment	trin'ket
trea'ty	tri'o
treb'le	trip
tree	tripe
trel'lis	trip'le
trem'ble	trip'lex
trem'bled	trip'licate, n. a.
trem'bling	trip'licate, v.
tremen'dous	trite
trem'or	trite'ly
trem'ulous	trite'ness
trench	tri'umph
trench'ant	trium'phal
trend	trium'phant
tres'pass	trium'phantly
tres'passed	tri'umphed
tres'passer	triv'ial
tres'passing	trivial'ity
tress	trod
tri'al	trodd'en
tri'angle	trol'ley
trian'gular	troop
	troop'er

tro'phy		try	
trop'ical		try'ing	
trot		try'-*on*	
trot'ted		tryst	
trot'ting		tub	
troub'le		tube	
troub'led		tuber'cular	
troub'lesome		tuberculo'sis	
troub'ling		tuber'culous	
troub'lous		tu'bing	
trough		tu'bular	
trou'sers		tuck	
trousseau'		Tu'dor	
trout		Tues'day	
trow'el		tuft	
tru'ant		tug	
truce		tui'tion	
truck		tu'lip	
tru'culence		tum'ble	
tru'culent		tum'bled	
trudge		tum'bler	
trudged		tu'mult	
trudg'ing		tumul'tuous	
true		tune	
tru'est		tuned	
tru'ism		tuneful	
trump		tune'fully	
trump'et		tu'ner	
trump'eter		tu'nic	
trun'dle		tu'ning	
trunk		tun'nel	
trunk'-call		tur'bine	
truss		tur'bulent	
trust		turf	
trust'ed		Turk	
trustee'		tur'key	
trust'ful		tur'moil	
trust'fully		turn	
trust'ing		turned	
trust'ingly		turn'er	
trust'worthi- ness		turn'ing	
		turn'ing-point	
trust'worthy		tur'nip	
trust'y		turn'over	
truth		turn'stile	
truth'ful		turn'table	
truth'fulness		tur'pentine	
truths		tur'ret	

tur'tle	*two*-seater
tusk	*two*-some
tus'sle	ty'ing
tu'tor	type
tuto'rial	type'script
tu'tors	type'writer
twad'dle	type'writing
tweed	type'written
twee'zers	ty'phoid
twelfth	typhoon'
twelve	typ'ical
twen'tieth	typ'ified
twen'ty	typ'ify
twice	ty'pist
twig	
twi'light	typograph'ic
twill	typograph'ical
twin	
twine	typog'raphy
twinge	typol'ogy
twi'ning	tyran'nic
twin'kle	tyran'nical
twin'kled	tyran'nically
twin'kling	tyr'annize
twist	tyr'annized
twist'ed	tyr'annous
twist'ing	tyr'anny
twitch	ty'rant
two	tyre
two'fold	ty'ro
	ty'rotox'icon

U

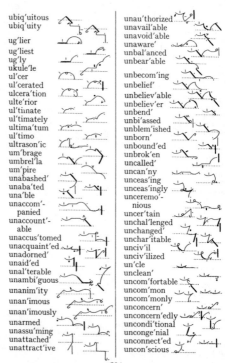

ubiq′uitous
ubiq′uity

ug′lier
ug′liest
ug′ly
ukule′le
ul′cer
ul′cerated
ulcera′tion
ulte′rior
ul′tinate
ul′timately
ultima′tum
ul′timo
ultrason′ic
um′brage
umbrel′la
um′pire
unabashed′
unaba′ted
una′ble
unaccom′-
    panied
unaccount′-
    able
unaccus′tomed
unacquaint′ed
unadorned′
unaid′ed
unal′terable
unambi′guous
unanim′ity
unan′imous
unan′imously
unarmed′
unassu′ming
unattached′
unattract′ive

unau′thorized
unavail′able
unavoid′able
unaware′
unbal′anced
unbear′able

unbecom′ing
unbelief′
unbeliev′able
unbeliev′er
unbend′
unbi′assed
unblem′ished
unborn′
unbound′ed
unbrok′en
uncalled′
uncan′ny
unceas′ing
unceas′ingly
unceremo′-
    nious
uncer′tain
unchal′lenged
unchanged′
unchar′itable
unciv′il
unciv′ilized
un′cle
unclean′
uncom′fortable
uncom′mon
uncom′monly
unconcern′
unconcern′edly
uncondi′tional
unconge′nial
unconnect′ed
uncon′scious

204

unconstitu'-
tional

unconstitu'-
tionally

uncontrol'lable

uncontrolled'

unconven'tional

uncouth'

uncov'er

uncul'tivated

uncut'

unda'ted

undaunt'ed

undeci'ded

undefend'ed

undefiled'

undefined'

undeliv'ered

undeni'able

un'der

un'dercarriage

un'dercoat

un'dercurrent

un'derdog

under-
es'timate, *n.*

under-
es'timate, *v.*

under-
es'timated

undergo'

undergrad'uate

un'derground

un'dergrowth

un'derhand

underline'

underly'ing

underneath'

un'der-
nourished

un'derpass

un'der-
pri'vileged

underrate'

under-
sec'retary

un'derstaffed

understand'

understate'ment

understood'

un'derstudy

undertake'

un'dertone

un'derwear

un'derworld

un'derwriter

undeserved'

undesir'able

undeterred'

undisclosed'

undisturbed'

undivi'ded

undo'

undoubt'ed

undoubt'edly

undress'

undue'

un'dulating

undu'ly

unearned'

uneas'ily

uneas'y

uneconom'ic

unemploy'able

unemployed'

unemploy'-
ment

une'qual

une'qualled

uner'ring

uner'ringly

une'ven

une'venly

unevent'ful

unexam'pled

unexpect'ed

unexpect'edly

unfail'ing

unfair'

unfaith'ful

unfamil'iar

unfash'ionable

unfa'vourable

unfeel'ing

unfeigned'	u'nison
unfert'ilized	u'nit
unfin'ished	unite'
unfit'	uni'ted
unflag'ging	u'nity
unflat'tering	univer'sal
unfold'	universal'ity
unforeseen'	univer'sally
unforgett'able	u'niverse
unfor'tunate	univer'sity
unfor'tunately	unjust'
unfound'ed	unjust'ifiable
unfriend'ly	unjus'tified
unfulfilled'	unkind'
unfurl'	unknown'
unfurled'	unlaw'ful
unfur'nished	unless'
ungen'tlemanly	unlike'
ungov'ernable	unlike'ly
ungra'cious	unlim'ited
ungrate'ful	unload'
unguard'ed	unlock'
unhap'pily	unluck'ily
unhap'py	unluck'y
unharmed'	unman'nerly
	unmind'ful
unhealth'y	unmista'kable
unhes'itatingly	
unhook'	unmit'igated
unhurt'	unmoved'
unhygien'ic	unnat'ural
uni'fied	unnec'essarily
u'niform	unnec'essary
uniform'ity	unno'ticed
	unobtain'able
u'niformly	unoffi'cial
u'nify	
unilat'eral	unor'ganized
unimpaired'	
	unorth'odox
unimpor'tant	unpaid'
unin'fluenced	unpal'atable
uninformed'	
unintel'ligible	unpar'alleled
uninten'tional	
uninterrupt'ed	unpleas'ant
u'nion	unpleas'antly
U'nionist	unpop'ular
unique'	unprec'edented
	unprej'udiced

unpremed'ita-
  ted
unprepared'
unprin'cipled
unproduc'tive
unprof'itable
unprotect'ed
unprovoked'
unpub'lished
unqual'ified
unques'tion-
  able
unques'tion-
  ably
unrav'el

unre'alizable
unrea'sonable
unrelat'ed
unreli'able
unremu'nera-
  tive
unrepresent'ed

unreserv'edly
unrest'
unrestrict'ed
unru'ly
unsafe'
unsatisfac'tory
unscrew'
unscrewed'

unscru'pulous
unseen'
unself'ish
unself'ishly
unself'ishness
unset'tle
unset'tled
unsight'ed
unsight'ly
unskil'ful

unskilled'
unso'ciable
unsoiled'
unsold'
unsolic'ited

unsophis'tica-
  ted
unsound'
unsound'ly
unspa'ring
unspa'ringly
unspe'cified
unsta'ble
unstead'ily
unstead'y
unstud'ied

unsuccess'ful
unsuccess'fully
unsuit'able
unsurpassed'
unsuspect'ed
unsuspect'ing

unswerv'ing
unsympathet'ic

untaxed'
unti'diness
unti'dy
untie'
untied'
until'
untime'ly
untir'ing
un'to
untold'

untoward'
untried'
untrod'den
untrue'
untruth'
unu'sual
unu'sually
unva'rying
unveil'
unwar'rantable

unwar'ranted

unwea'ried

unwel'come
unwell'

unwhole'some

unwield'y	
unwil'ling	
unwil'lingly	
unwise'	
unwise'ly	
unwit'tingly	
unwork'able	
unwor'thy	
unwrit'ten	
unyield'ing	
up	
up'bringing	
upheav'al	
upheave'	
upheld'	
uphill'	
uphold'	
uphold'ing	
uphol'ster	
uphol'sterer	
uphol'stery	
uplift'	
upon'	
up'per	
up'permost	
up'right'	
up'roar	
uproar'ious	
uproot'	
upset'	
up'surge	
up'swing	
up'wards	
ur'ban	
urbane'	
urban'ity	
ur'chin	
urge	
ur'gency	

ur'gent	
ur'gently	
urn	
us	
u'sable	
u'sage	
use	
used	
use'ful	
use'fully	
use'fulness	
use'less	
use'lessly	
use'lessness	
u'ser	
ush'er	
ush'ered	
usherette'	
u'sing	
u'sual	
u'sually	
u'surer	
usurp'	
u'sury	
uten'sil	
util'ity	
utiliza'tion	
u'tilize	
u'tilized	
u'tilizing	
ut'most	
Uto'pia	
ut'ter	
ut'terance	
ut'tered	
ut'tering	
ut'terly	
ut'termost	
u'vula	

V

va'cancy
va'cant
vacate'
vaca'ted
vaca'ting
vaca'tion
vac'cinate
vac'cinated
vaccina'tion
vac'cine
vac'illate
vac'illated
vac'illating
vacilla'tion
vac'uous
vac'uum
vag'abond
vaga'ry
va'grancy
va'grant
vague
vague'ly
vain
vain'ly
vale
valedic'tory
val'ency
val'et
val'iant
val'iantly
val'id
val'idate
valid'ity
valise'
val'ley
val'orous
val'our
val'uable
valua'tion
val'ue

val'ued
valve
valv'ular
vamp
vam'pire
van
vanil'la
van'ish
van'ished
van'ishing
van'ity
van'quish
van'tage
vap'id
vap'orizer
va'pour,
   va'por
va'riable
va'riance
va'riant
varia'tion
va'ried
vari'ety
va'rious
var'nish
var'nishing
va'ry
va'rying
vase
Vas'eline
vas'sal
vast
vast'ly
vat
Vat'ican
vaude'ville
vault
vault'ed
vault'ing
vaunt

vaunt'ed	
veal	
veer	
veered	
veer'ing	
veg'etable	
vegeta'rian	
vegeta'rianism	
veg'etate	
vegeta'tion	
ve'hemence	
ve'hement	
ve'hemently	
ve'hicle	
vehic'ular	
veil	
veiled	
vein	
vel'lum	
veloc'ity	
velour'	
vel'vet	
velveteen'	
vend'er, vend'or	
vendet'ta	
vend'or (legal term)	
veneer'	
ven'erable	
ven'erate	
venera'tion	
Vene'tian	
ven'geance	
ve'nial	
ven'ison	
ven'om	
ven'omous	
vent	
ven'tilate	
ven'tilated	
ventila'tion	
ven'tilator	
ven'ture	
ven'tured	
ven'turesome	
ven'turing	

ven'ue	
vera'cious	
verac'ity	
veran'dah	
verb	
ver'bal	
verba'tim	
ver'biage	
verbose'	
verbos'ity	
ver'dant	
ver'dict	
ver'dure	
verge	
verifica'tion	
ver'ified	
ver'ify	
ver'ily	
ver'itable	
vermil'ion	
ver'min	
ver'satile	
versatil'ity	
verse	
ver'sion	
ver'sus	
ver'tebrae	
ver'tical	
ver'y	
ves'sel	
vest	
vest'ed	
ves'tibule	
ves'tige	
vest'ment	
ves'try	
ves'ture	
vet'eran	
vet'erinary	
ve'to	
vex	
vexa'tion	
vexa'tious	
vexed	
vi'a	
vi'aduct	
vi'al	
vi'brant	

vi′brate		viola′tion	
vi′brated		vi′olence	
vibra′tion		vi′olent	
vic′ar		vi′olently	
vica′rious		vi′olet	
vice		violin′	
vice-chair′man		violin′ist	
vice-pres′ident		vi′per	
vice-prin′cipal		vir′gin	
		vir′ile	
vic′e ver′sa		viril′ity	
vicin′ity		vir′tual	
vic′ious		vir′tue	
vic′iously		virtuos′ity	
vicis′situde		vir′tuous	
vic′tim		vir′ulence	
victimiza′tion		vir′ulent	
vic′tor		vi′sa	
victo′rious		vis′age	
vic′tory		vis′cous	
vict′uals		vi′sé	
vid′eo		visibil′ity	
vie		vis′ible	
view		vi′sion	
viewed		vi′sionary	
vig′il		vis′it	
vig′ilance		visita′tion	
vig′ilant		vis′ited	
vig′orous		vis′iting	
vig′our		vis′itor	
vile		vis′ta	
vil′la		vis′ual	
vil′lage		visualiza′tion	
vil′lain		vis′ualize	
vil′lainous		vi′tal	
vil′lainy		vital′ity	
vim		vi′tally	
vin′dicate		vi′tamin	
vin′dicated		vi′tiate	
vindica′tion		vi′tiated	
vindic′tive		vitriol′ic	
vindic′tively		vitu′perate	
vine		vitupera′tion	
vin′egar		viva′cious	
vine′yard		vivac′ity	
vin′tage		viv′id	
vi′olate		viv′idly	
vi′olated		vivisec′tion	

vocab'ulary
vo'cal
vo'calist
vocaliza'tion
vcca'tion
voca'tional
vocif'erous
vod'ka
vogue
voice
void
vol'atile
vol'-au-vent'

volcan'ic

volca'no
vol'ley
volt
volt'age
volubil'ity
vol'uble
vol'ume
volu'minous
vol'untarily
vol'untary

volunteer'
volunteered'
volunteer'ing
vora'cious
vo'tary
vote
vo'ted
vo'ter
vouch
vouch'er
vouchsafe
vow
vowed
vow'el
voy'age
vul'canite

vul'canize
vul'gar
vulgar'ity
vul'garly
vulnerabil'ity
vul'nerable
vul'ture
vy'ing

W

wad
wad'ding
wade
wa'ded
wa'ding
wa'fer
waf'fle
waft
waft'ed
wag
wage
wage'-freeze
wa'ger
wag'on,
    wag'gon
waif
wail
wailed
wain'scot
wain'scotting
waist
waist'coat
wait
wait'ed
wait'er
wait'ing-list
wait'ing-room
wait'ress
waive
wake
wake'ful
wake'fulness
wa'ken
wa'kening
walk
walked
walk'er
walk'ing
walk'ing-stick
walk'-out

walk'-over
wall
wal'let
wal'low
wall'paper
wal'nut
wal'rus
waltz
waltzed
wan
wand
wan'der
wan'dered
wan'derer
wan'dering
wane
want
want'ed
wan'ton
war
war'ble
ward
ward'en
ward'er
ward'robe
ware'house
wares
war'fare
war'ily
war'like
warm
warmed
warm'er
warm'est
warm'-hearted
warmth
warn
warned
warn'ing
warn'ingly

213

warp	way'faring
war'rant	way'side
war'ranted	*we*
war'ranty	weak
war'rior	weak'en
war'ship	weak'er
wa'ry	weak'ness
was	weal
wash	wealth
wash'able	wealth'ier
washed	wealth'iest
wash'er	wealth'y
wash'ing	weap'on
wash'out	wear
wasp	wear'able
waste	wear'er
wast'ed	wear'ied
waste'ful	wear'ing
waste'fully	wear'isome
wa'sting	wear'y
watch	wear'ying
watched	weath'er
watch'er	weath'erproof
watch'ful	weave
watch'fulness	weav'er
watch'ing	weav'ing
watch'man	web
wa'ter	wed'ding
wa'terfall	wedge
wa'terfront	wedged
	wedg'ing
wa'termark	Wednes'day
	weed
wa'termelon	week
wa'terproof	week'day
wa'tershed	week-end'
wa'tertight	week'ly
watt	weep
wave	weigh
waved	weighed
wave'length	weigh'ing
wa'ver	weight
wa'vered	weight'y
wa'vering	weir
wa'ving	weird
wa'vy	wel'come
wax	wel'comed
way	wel'coming
way'farer	

weld		*which*	
weld'ed		*which*ev'er	
weld'ing		whiff	
wel'fare		while	
well		whiled	
well-known'		whilst	
well-mean'ing		whim	
Welsh		whim'per	
wel'ter		whim'pered	
went		whim'pering	
wept		whim'sical	
were		whine	
west		whined	
west'erly		whi'ning	
west'ern		whip	
west'ward		whirl	
wet		whirled	
whale		whirl'ing	
wharf		whirl'pool	
wharf'age		whirl'wind	
what		whis'key,	
what'ever		whis'ky	
whatsoev'er		whis'per	
wheat		whis'pered	
wheel		whis'pering	
wheel'-base		whist	
wheeled		whis'tle	
when		whis'tled	
whence		whit	
whenev'er		white	
whensoev'er		whith'er	
where		whithersoev'er	
where'abouts		whit'tle	
whereas'		whiz	
whereat'		*who*	
whereby'		*who*ev'er	
where'fore		whole	
where'*in*		whole'heart'ed	
where*in*soev'er		whole- heart'edly	
where*of'*		whole'sale	
where*on'*		whole'some	
wheresoev'er		whol'ly	
where*to'*		whom	
whereupon'		whoop	
wherev'er		whose	
wherewithal'		whosoev'er	
wheth'er		why	

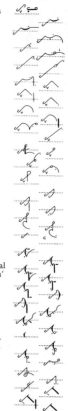

wick	wine'-glass
wick'ed	wing
wick'er	wink
wick'et	win'ner
wide	win'ning
wide'ly	win'some
wi'den	win'ter
wi'dened	win'terly
wi'dening	win'try
wi'der	wipe
wide'spread	wiped
wid'ow	wi'ping
wid'ower	wire
width	wired
wield	wire'less
wife	wir'y
wig	wis'dom
wild	wise
wild'er	wise'ly
wil'derness	wi'ser
wild'est	wi'sest
wild'ly	wish
wile	wished
wil'ful	wish'ing
wil'fully	wist'ful
wil'fulness	wist'fully
will	wit
willed	*with*
will'ing	withal'
wil'lingly	withdraw'
wil'low	withdraw'al
wilt	withdrawn'
wi'ly	withdrew'
win	with'er
wince	with'ered
winced	withheld'
wind, *n.*	withhold'
wind, *v.*	within'
wind'fall	*without'*
wind'ing	withstand'
win'dow	withstood'
win'dow-dressing	wit'ness
wind'screen	wit'ticism
wind'-tunnel	wit'ty
wind'ward	wiz'ard
wine	wob'ble
wine'-cellar	wob'bled
	wob'bling

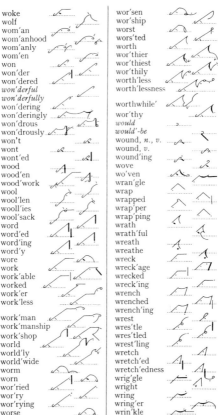

woke	wor'sen
wolf	wor'ship
wom'an	worst
wom'anhood	wors'ted
wom'anly	worth
wom'en	wor'thier
won	wor'thiest
won'der	wor'thily
won'dered	worth'less
won'derful	worth'lessness
won'derfully	
won'dering	worthwhile'
won'deringly	wor'thy
won'drous	*would*
won'drously	*would'-be*
won't	wound, *n., v.*
wont	wound, *v.*
wont'ed	wound'ing
wood	wove
wood'en	wo'ven
wood'work	wran'gle
wool	wrap
wool'len	wrapped
wooll'ies	wrap'per
wool'sack	wrap'ping
word	wrath
word'ed	wrath'ful
word'ing	wreath
word'y	wreathe
wore	wreck
work	wreck'age
work'able	wrecked
worked	wreck'ing
work'er	wrench
work'less	wrenched
	wrench'ing
work'man	wrest
work'manship	wres'tle
work'shop	wres'tled
world	wrest'ling
world'ly	wretch
world'wide	wretch'ed
worm	wretch'edness
worn	wrig'gle
wor'ried	wright
wor'ry	wring
wor'rying	wring'er
worse	wrin'kle

wrist	wrong
wrist'let	wronged
wrist'watch	wrong'ful
writ	wrong'fully
write	wrong'ly
wri'ter	wrote
write'-up	wroth
writhe	wrought'
writhed	wrought'-iron'
wri'ting	wrung
writ'ten	wry

X

xan'thium
xantho-
 car'pous
xe'nial
xenog'amy
xenoglos'(s)ia
xen'on
xenophob'ia
xera'sia
xero'graphy
xeroph'agy
xerophthal'mia

xero'sis

xiph'oid
X-ray'
X-rays
xy'lem
xy'locarp
xy'lograph
xy'loid
xyloi'din(e)
xylom'eter
xy'lonite
xyloph'agous
xy'lophone
xys'ter
xys'tus

Y

yacht
yacht'ing
yank
yard
yarn
yawn
yawned
yawn'ing
ye
yea
year
year'-book
year'ly

yearn
yearned
yearn'ing
yeast
yell
yel'low
yelp
yelped
yelp'ing
yes
yes'terday

yet
yew
Yid'dish
yield
yield'ed
yo'ghourt
yoke
yo'kel
yolk
yon'der
you
young
young'er
young'est
young'ster
your
*your*self'
*your*selves'
youth
youth'ful
youth'-
  fulness
youths
Yule
Yule'tide

Z

zaʹny
zapʹtieh
zareʹba

zarʹnich
zax
zeʹa
zeal
zealʹot
zealʹous
zealʹously
zeʹbra
zed
zedʹoary
zeitʹgeist
zen
zenʹith
zephʹyr
zeʹro
zest
zestʹful
zigʹzag
zinc
zinʹnia
zip
zipʹ-fasʹtener

zirʹcon
zithʹer
zoʹdiac
zoʹnal
zone
zoʹning
zoologʹical
zoolʹogist
zoolʹogy
zoom
Zuʹlu
zyʹgal
zygodacʹtyl
zygoʹma
zygomatʹic
zygʹote
zyme
zymolʹogist
zymolʹogy
zymomʹeter
zyʹmoscope
zymoʹsis
zymotʹic
zyʹmurgy
zyʹthum
zyxomʹma